A DOSE OF SALTS

A Dose of Salts

Simon Coupland

MONARCH

Crowborough

British Library Cataloguing Data
A catalogue record for this book is available
from the British Library.

ISBN 1 85424 384 5

Designed and produced by Bookprint Creative Services
P.O. Box 827, BN21 3YJ, England for
MONARCH PUBLICATIONS
Broadway House, The Broadway,
Crowborough, East Sussex, TN6 1HQ.
Printed in Great Britain.

CONTENTS

INTRODUCTION

'AND FATHER, I ask thee now for a good text to accompany this fantastic joke.' So ran the caption to a cartoon of a praying preacher in *Leadership* magazine in Winter 1989. If I am honest, I must admit that there have been times when I have been tempted to twist a sermon or talk in a direction I hadn't previously intended, in order to include an especially memorable illustration. On reflection, the reason I felt I needed to do this was because I didn't have an illustration to reinforce the point I wanted to make. So the solution was: more illustrations!

It was reputedly Queen Victoria (another version says Abraham Lincoln – which suggests it was neither!) who said that if all the people who fell asleep in church were laid end to end along the pews, they would be a lot more comfortable. We *need* stories – whether they be jokes, anecdotes, illustrations, testimonies or accounts of remarkable events – to help our listeners to listen. You can often detect the slight change in a speaker's voice when he or she starts telling a story, and you can also see the immediate effect on the audience. People sit up and prick up their ears, and as a number of the stories in this book reveal, that makes a big change for some (see under 'Boredom' in the Index). I do not believe it was a coincidence that Jesus ended a number of his stories with the saying, 'Whoever has ears to hear, let them hear' (Mt 13:9, 43; Mk 4:23; Lk 14:35). People listen to stories, even in this very visual culture, and if we as speakers have something to say which we think is worth saying, we need to help our listeners to hear it. We can learn from firms which send out junk mail, that bane of modern life. They have discovered that to hook a customer you need AIDA. Nothing to do with Verdi, but Attention, Interest, Desire, Action. If you want to get people to act on what you say, you first need to grab their attention and then retain their interest. This book is intended to help.

That prompts another thought. Sometimes we speakers worry that people remember the stories we tell, but not the point they were intended to illustrate. One way round this is by using illustrations which make the point in themselves, such as the story of the Japanese village transformed by the Bible (story no. 37), or the fact that humans are no more than a collection of chemicals (story no. 135). But here we do well to remember AIDA again: sometimes a story serves simply to capture people's attention. That well-worn routine of telling a joke at the beginning of a sermon, for instance, often serves the purpose of making people listen to what follows, and that is all the preacher asks. Of course, it helps if another illustration is included a few minutes later, or the effect is all too rapidly lost.

Of course we should use our own illustrations, which don't come from books. In particular, we should draw on personal and topical material, from our own experience or from current events. Everybody knows about recent disasters similar to the one in Siloam where a tower collapsed, killing a number of people (Lk 13:4) so it's good to refer to them. But such occurrences won't usually find their way into a collection like this. Having said that, many of the stories here come from ephemeral sources: newspapers and magazines. That is partly deliberate, since books remain available and accessible for much longer while news reports are swiftly forgotten. It has also been my conscious decision to avoid reproducing material that has already been included in other collections, such as the books by Murray Watts or Graham Twelftree.

I have done my best to acknowledge the sources of all the material in this book, either the publication in which I read it or the speaker from whom I heard it, even if the chances are that the story may well have originated somewhere else. If I have failed to acknowledge a source accurately or adequately, please accept my apologies and do put me right by way of the publishers.

Finally, I would like to express my thanks to Tony and Jane Collins at Monarch, for paying attention to a letter out of the blue, and acting upon it. And above all, my thanks to my wife Heather, my most faithful friend and constructive critic, for accepting the hours of enforced absence in the study. This book is dedicated, with my love, to her.

GOD

1. A child's view

(Animals, Death, Food, Justice, Suffering, Theology, Humour)

Katie Lee, a six-year-old from North London, obviously thought a lot about God. 'There's one God,' she said, 'and he's the creator of heaven. God is Jesus' father. God has glasses, I think. I don't think God has animals in the air. I think God has animals on the ground and he comes down and feeds them. I think God has not got a cooker in the air. He comes down and has takeaways. He tries lots of different sorts because there's lots of people in the world. God likes Indian and Japanese but I think he likes McDonalds best. I think he has coffee to keep him warm.'

'He is normally fair, but sometimes not. Daddy's secretary was only twenty-nine and she died in a car crash. Why wasn't God looking?'

Bible references: Genesis 18:25; Deuteronomy 32:4; Job 36:31; Psalm 104:14, 21, 27-8; 145:15; 147:9; Jeremiah 12:1.

Source: Adapted from the *Sunday Times*, 17 April 1983.

2. Defining the Deity

(Agnostics, Belief, Charity, Doctrine, Hell, Holy Communion, Humanism, Inland Revenue, Prayer, Religion, Tax, Humour)

In 1979, the British Inland Revenue was faced with a tricky theological question: how do you define God? It was all the fault of a small organisation called the South Place Ethical Society, formed in 1793 as an offshoot of the American Universalist Church. This was basically Christian, except that they had cut out eternal damnation because it didn't seem reasonable. In 1869 they dropped intercessory prayer, and Holy Communion not long after that. At some point belief in God was dispensed with as well, so by 1979 the Society consisted of 689 agnostics and humanists who put on classical concerts and lectures on matters of moral concern.

And therein lay the problem. The Society still claimed tax exemption as a religious charity, but the Inland Revenue argued that if they no longer believed in God, they were by definition no longer a religious organisation. For their part, the Society claimed that truth, love and beauty were in themselves proper objects of religious contemplation, even when they were unrelated to any supernatural being. 'Our services are Christian in format, but all references to God have been deleted,' said a spokesman. 'After all, most church ministers stopped believing in God years ago.'

Source: Adapted from the *Sunday Telegraph*, 18 March 1979.

3. The Father's presence

(Child of God, Children, Courage, Fear, Love, Manhood, Presence of God, Protection, Sons)

In one particular tribe in India, it was the custom that on a boy's thirteenth birthday he had to spend the night on his own in the depths of the jungle. This was the tribe's rite of passage from boyhood: pass this test, and you had proved that you were a true man. The fateful night came for one young man. Every sound made him jump; every animal cry caused him to tremble, and more than once he thought about giving up and making his way back to the safety of his village. But he stayed, and gradually through the thick tangle of trees the first rays of light began to herald the coming of morning.

As the light grew stronger and the young man began to make out the shapes around him, he was astonished to see the figure of his father, not far away, a gun by his side. All night long he had been there keeping guard, watching over his son to make sure that no harm befell him. And the son thought to himself, 'If only I had known that my father was there, I wouldn't have been frightened at all!'

Bible references: Psalm 7:1-2; 16; 17; 18; 23:4; 33:12-21; 34; 57:1-4; 91; 121; Matthew 10:28-31; Luke 12:4-7; John 17:15.

Source: Adapted from James A. Feehan, *Preaching in Stories* (The Mercier Press, 1989), p 62.

4. Finding favour

(Commitment, Commuting, Faith, Opposition, Popularity, Trains, the World)

It was a very cold winter's day, and the commuters on the Victoria train were glad that the heating was working in their carriages. The train pulled into the station, coats and scarves were pulled on, and they flooded out onto the platform. At the barrier there was a ticket inspector calling out 'All season tickets, please!' A queue built up, and people grumbled as the cold air seeped into their warm clothing while they searched out their tickets. As one passenger reached the ticket inspector, he said, 'You're not very popular today, you know.' Pointing towards the British Rail offices, the man replied, 'As long as I'm popular up there, chum, I don't mind what people think down here.'

Bible references: Isaiah 8:12-13; 51:7-8; Matthew 10:28; Luke 12:4-5; Romans 12:1-2; 1 John 2:15.

Source: Adapted from Peter Sertin, Paris, 12 October 1980.

5. The Glory of God

(Creation, Faith, Judaism, Other faiths, Rabbis)

A pagan emperor once visited the famed Jewish rabbi, Joshua ben Hananiah, and asked to be shown the rabbi's God. Joshua answered that this was impossible, but this reply failed to satisfy the emperor who continued to insist that he be allowed to see the God of Israel. So the rabbi took the emperor outside and told him to stare into the midday sun. 'But that's impossible!' replied the emperor. 'If you cannot look at the sun, which God created,' retorted rabbi Joshua, 'how much less can you behold the glory of God himself?'

Bible references: Exodus 3:6; 20:19; Deuteronomy 5:24-6; 18:16; John 1:14; 11:40; Acts 7:55; 2 Corinthians 3:7, 18; 4:4-6; Revelation 21:23.

Source: Quoted in Alister McGrath, *Understanding the Trinity* (Kingsway, 1987), pp 46-7.

6. The Holy Spirit

(Bible, Comforter, Counsellor, Helper, Paraclete, Translation)

Some years ago, the Bible Society were working on a translation of John's Gospel into the Karré language, which is spoken in equatorial Africa. They had reached chapter 14 and were looking for the local word to describe the paraclete: a comforter, helper or the like. To their surprise and delight they found the perfect equivalent. In the local culture, if one of a line of porters becomes exhausted from carrying his heavy load, and another bends down to help him up, he is known in Karré as 'the one who falls down beside us' – a wonderful picture of the work of the Spirit.

Bible references: John 14:16, 26; 15:26; 16:7; 1 John 2:1.

Source: Adapted from Robert Paterson, *Short, Sharp and Off the Point* (MARC Europe, 1987), p 101.

7. The Incarnation

(Christ, Christmas, Humility, Jesus)

Like your landlord becoming your lodger;
Like your managing director up before you for an
  interview;
Like Beethoven queuing up for a ticket to his own concert;
Like a headmaster getting the cane;
Like a good architect living in a slum built by a rival;
Like Picasso painting by numbers –
God lived among us.

Bible references: Matthew 1:18-25; 20:28; Mark 10:45; Luke
1-2; John 1:1-14; 13:3-12; 2 Corinthians 8:9; Philippians 2:5-
11; Hebrews 5:8.

Source: David Watson, *Jesus Then and Now*: the video (Lella
Productions).

8. Judgement

*(Children, Families, Fear, Food, Fussiness, Parenthood,
Punishment, Storms, Threats, Humour)*

Little Trevor was a good boy on the whole, but the one thing
that made his mum cross was his fussiness about food. She
tried hard to make him eat what the rest of the family ate, but
all too often he refused. One day they were having prunes for
tea, but Trevor would have none. She pleaded with him, she
promised him treats, she threatened him with going straight to
bed, and in the end, in sheer exasperation, she shouted,

'Trevor, God will be very cross with you if you don't eat your prunes!' But Trevor still refused, and so off he went to bed.

That night there was a terrible storm: the lightning flashed, the thunder crashed, and mum was a bit worried about little Trevor. She went up to his room, but he wasn't in his bed. She looked in the bathroom, in her bedroom, and then finally spotted the light on in the kitchen. As she walked in, there was Trevor in front of the fridge, eating his bowl of prunes, and she heard him mutter, 'I don't know, God. What a lot of fuss to make about a few prunes!'

Bible references: Luke 13:2; John 9:2; Acts 28:4; Hebrews 12:18-24; 1 John 4:18.

Source: unknown.

9. Science and God

(Creation, Evolution, Music, Mystery, Myth, Stories, Truth)

There was once a family of mice who lived in a piano. They loved the music which flooded through their house day after day, but often wondered where it came from. Some said that you only had to hear the beauty of the music to realise that there must be a player who was making it. But others scoffed at the idea, and came up with alternative theories of their own.

Then one day a brave and very daring mouse decided to find out for himself where the music was coming from. He set out from their snug little den and explored the great, dark recesses of the piano's interior. And there he discovered the source of the music: it was the strings! He raced back to the family and told them of his discovery. Now they knew – or did they? Because of course some questioned whether the brave explorer was really right – indeed whether he was telling the truth.

So a little while later another expedition set out, this time consisting of several mice so that there could be no question of their honesty. Sure enough, they found the strings which the first mouse had described. But they decided to press on still further, and there they discovered the secret of the strings – the secret behind the secret. For what really made the music in the piano was – the hammers.

Now the mice understood everything. There was no longer any mystery about the origin of the music. And they laughed at the elderly mice who sometimes still told the old stories about the piano player. And, unseen by them all, the piano player played on.

Bible references: Isaiah 19:11-12; 29:14; 44:24-5; Jeremiah 8:8-9; Romans 1:20-3; 1 Corinthians 1:18-25; 2:6-8; 2 Corinthians 4:4.

Source: Adapted from Andrew Briggs, Cambridge 1979.

10. A smile on the face of God

(Bigotry, Children, Desegregation, Faith, Intolerance, Presence of God, Racism)

The year was 1962, and in the United States, racial tension was high. An eight-year-old black girl from North Carolina found herself in the middle of a mob of white people protesting against the desegregation of schools. She said, 'I was alone, and those people were screaming, and suddenly I saw God smiling, and I smiled. A woman was standing near the school door, and she shouted at me, "Hey, you little nigger, what you smiling at?" I looked right at her face, and I said, "At God." She looked up at the sky, and then she looked at me, and she didn't call me any more names.'

Bible references: Exodus 33:11; Numbers 6:25-6; Matthew 11:25-6; 18:2-3, 10; 19:13-14; 21:15-16; Mark 9:36-7; 10:13-16; Luke 10:21; 18:16; Acts 6:15; Revelation 22:4.

Source: Quoted in review of Robert Coles, 'The Spiritual Life of Children' in *Christianity Today*, 7 October 1991.

11. The Trinity

(Fines, Local government, Money, Tax, Humour)

Lambeth Council in London was forced to admit that it had sent three demands for Council Tax to the church of St John the Divine in Brixton, addressed to God the Father, God the Son and God the Holy Ghost respectively. Each was asked to pay the sum of £521, or face possible court action. In its defence, the council said that it was hard for their staff to weed out frivolous applications.

Bible references: Matthew 17:24-7; 22:15-21; Mark 12:13-17; Luke 20:20-6; Romans 13:6-7.

Source: *Have I Got News For You* (BBC Books, 1994).

12. The Trinity

(Doctrine, Faith, Films, Holy Spirit, Jesus, Nuns, Religion, Roman Catholics, Theology, Humour)

In the film *Nuns on the Run*, lapsed Catholic Robbie Coltrane tries to explain the doctrine of the Trinity to the unchurched Eric Idle.

RC: Here's the pitch. You've got the Father, the Son and the Holy Ghost. The three are one, like a shamrock, my old priest used to say. Three leafs, but one leaf. Now the Father sent down the Son, who was love, and then when he went away, he sent the Holy Spirit, who came down in the form of a...

EI [interrupts]: You've told me already, a ghost.

RC: No, a dove.

EI: The dove was a ghost?

RC: No, the Ghost was a dove.

EI: Let me try and summarise this. God is his Son, and his Son is God, but his Son moonlights as a Holy Ghost, a Holy Spirit, and a dove, and they all sent each other, even though they're all one and the same thing.

RC: You've got it. You really could be a nun.

EI: Wait a minute. What I said – does that make any sense to you?

RC: Oh no, but it makes no sense to anybody. That's why you have to believe it. That's why you have to have faith. If it made sense, it wouldn't have to be a religion, would it?

Bible references: Matthew 3:13-17; Mark 1:9-11; Luke 3:21-2; 24:49; John 1:31-4; 14:23-6; 15:26; 16:5-7; Romans 8:3;

Galatians 4:4-6; Hebrews 11:1.

Source: *Nuns on the Run* (HandMade Films, 1990).

GOOD NEWS

13. Conversion: Andy Maycock's story

(Alpha, Child of God, Christianity, Disability, Faith, God, Hell, Religion, Suffering, Testimony)

Andy Maycock has had cerebral palsy since birth. He was brought up as a Christian, but didn't accept it for himself. He knew all the theory, but saw it as a harsh religion based on reward and punishment: 'If you were a naughty boy you went to hell, and if you were a good boy you didn't.' But then in 1995 he went on an Alpha course at Banbury Baptist Church in Oxfordshire, where suddenly he saw Christianity from a very different perspective, and it all made sense. One consequence was that it totally changed his attitude towards his disability. He said, 'I used to think, "How can there be a God if I am like I am? How dare he make me like I am?" But really, adversity and suffering bring love and caring, and sharing and understanding. I have learned a lot. I'm glad I have got the opportunity to look at things like Jesus did. He suffered. He had adversity. But look how much he loved. Now I have got to learn to try and be like that.

'Jesus has changed me from being a victim of circumstances into the son of a King. I may still be crippled on the outside but I'm no longer crippled on the inside. This is one bubble that is never going to burst.'

Bible references: John 1:12-13; Romans 5:3; 8:14-23; Galatians 3:26; 4:4-6; Hebrews 2:17-18; 5:8-9; 1 Peter 4:19.

Source: Adapted from *Alpha News*, December 1995.

14. Conversion: Cabo Bruno's story

(Bible, Bible study, Crime, Cruelty, Forgiveness, Hope, Murder, Peace, Prison, Repentance, Salvation, Suicide, Testimony, Violence, Witness)

At the age of twenty, the Brazilian 'Cabo' Bruno became a military policeman in São Paolo. He saw the terrible conditions of the favela slums, and the way in which the inhabitants were victimised by criminals. He says he joined the police to execute justice, to hit back at the criminals: 'I ended up fighting unscrupulous people. I performed wicked things.' As the bodies of murdered criminals began to turn up near where the policeman lived, rumours spread that he was responsible. The newspapers dubbed him 'Corporal Cabo Bruno, the south-side killer.'

He was arrested, accused of six murders, and sent to the city's military prison. 'I couldn't get used to being in prison. I tried to escape using the only thing I knew: violence. During my escape one of the prison wardens reacted and I shot him. That was the first of my three escape attempts.' After his last escape and recapture, Bruno was sent to a maximum security prison, facing a sentence of over 100 years. 'As the heavy gate shut behind my back, I was sure I'd either die of grief or in the hands of my enemies. In my cell it was as if I'd been buried alive. Exhausted and abandoned, I blamed God for everything, and ached in despair. I couldn't see any light in the darkness that surrounded my life. Suicide was my only way out.'

Then a Bible arrived in the post, with a letter from a lady who had heard about him. She told Bruno that Jesus offered him a way out. So he started reading it, and 'I felt a great change taking place. The repentance was so deep in my heart that I cried all night, recalling the cruelties I'd executed. I wept in the presence of God. The light of hope shone, and unexpectedly life started making sense. God had shown me that with him I was being granted a new life. I understood that to be saved all I had to do was to confess my sins to the Lord, and invite Jesus Christ to enter my life. So I did, and I found life instead of death. Everything changed. I became filled with such an intense inner peace, deep relief, and with a great desire to live and to love.'

Soon Bruno began to share his new-found faith with other prisoners, and several of them became Christians too. He started leading Bible studies with those whose cells were nearby, but because they were not allowed to associate they had to lie on the floor and talk to each other through the gap under the door of their cells. He had now found a new purpose in life, saying, 'Today my prayer is for all to come to know God.'

Bible references: 1 Kings 8:22-53; 2 Chronicles 6:12-42; Psalm 51; 103; Proverbs 28:13; Isaiah 1:18; 55:6-11; Daniel 9:3-23; Acts 2:37-8; 16:23-34; Romans 1:16; 10:8-11; 1 John 1:9.

Source: Adapted from the Bible Society, *Word in Action 96*, issue 80, p 6.

15. Conversion: Martyn Harris' story

(Afterlife, Belief, Bible, Cancer, Church, Conversion, Death, Faith, Gospels, Jesus, Life, New Testament, Religion, Scepticism, Sickness, Testimony, Uncertainty)

In 1995, *Daily Telegraph* journalist Martyn Harris was told that he had cancer. By nature he was an atheist and by profession a cynic, but his illness, enforced idleness, the kindness of friends and strangers, and the prospect of death all combined to make him reconsider his views on Christianity. He wrote:

'I was brought up in the Methodist church but stopped going when I was fourteen or so, and refused to be confirmed. As an arrogant, would-be intellectual adolescent, I wanted to hear arguments about things that mattered, such as the existence of God, the truth of the resurrection and the problem of evil. I liked the pretty Welsh village chapel, founded by my ancestors, whose names were commemorated on tablets around the walls. But there wasn't much intellectual meat to be had in chapel: the ministers never seemed to deal with the basics of belief, instead making laboured attempts to draw up-to-date parallels with the Gospel stories. It was as if science and the modern world had terrorised religion out of tackling its own central mysteries.

'I couldn't help noticing that most of the congregation seemed to consist of old widowed ladies, and that such young people as there were always seemed to be the least attractive and most badly dressed types that one avoided at school. I concluded, with the cruel certainty of youth, that religion was for old people frightened of dying, and for young people who couldn't pull.

'Although I went to Sunday School until I was about fourteen, I am ashamed to say I had never read a single Gospel all the way through, though they are such slender things which you can get through in an hour or two. Still more grotesquely, I was embarrassed to be seen reading them, and would shuffle the Bible under some other book if anyone came into the room. Christians, after all, were people who knew nothing of Bob Dylan or Jarvis Cocker, who had fish signs on the back of their cars, and terrible taste in shoes. What would my friends think? Poor old Martyn; the cancer has made him go over to the God Squad. I was terrified that I might be running to religion out of fear, but there was a quote from Martin Luther which helped: "God uses lust to impel man to marry, ambition to office, avarice to earning and fear to faith. God led me like an old blind goat."

'In any case, I found I enjoyed the Gospels: the poetic compression of language; the suggestive and paradoxical thought patterns of the teaching; above all, the force and authority of Jesus' personality which comes scorching through. No fair-minded person could read these stories without acknowledging that here at the very least was a phenomenon in history, whose mere acquaintance drove ordinary men to sacrifice their homes and families and ultimately their lives to spread the story across the known world in a single generation. These were not the vaguely remembered children's stories of gentle Jesus meek n' mild but an account of spiritual transformation and revolution.

'Considered merely as literature – and that was just how I read it at first – the New Testament was extraordinary. I could go on for quite a long time here: about my surprise at the intellectual coherence of Christianity; at the feebleness of much of the materialist position which I had assumed to be so impregnable. But one of the things I have learned while writing this article, which has taken me longer and cost me more drafts than almost anything else I have written, is that ultimately you cannot simply argue yourself or anyone else into a faith. There is a quote from Dean Inge, "Faith begins as an experiment and ends as an experience". I believe the experience is there for anyone if you are desperate enough, as I have been, or open enough, or perhaps simple enough.

'The sense of a reality outside and beyond time, unifying and making sense of experience, is a matter of "hints and guesses", sometimes there, more often not. Sometimes I have been filled with well-being and serenity. Sometimes I am convinced it is nothing but self-delusion brought on by a terror of my own mortality, that the whole of religion is just what Philip Larkin suggested: a "vast moth-eaten musical brocade/ Created to pretend we never die."

'Nobody really knows what is "out there" beyond our death, beyond the stars, not Stephen Hawking or Richard Dawkins or Philip Larkin or the Rev. Billy Graham. All the ways we have of approaching our existence, from science to religion, are ultimately no more than models, and you have the power to choose your own. Larkin was a brave man in his way, but he chose a model which left him drunk, suicidal, self-obsessed and paralysed by misery. The scientific atheist who, like Richard Dawkins, sees life as the chance outcome of a cosmic singularity chooses a model which leaves him in an attitude of existential bravado, shouting his discoveries at the edge of a cooling and indifferent universe. As I sit here, looking at my fingers on the keyboard, smelling the wisteria flowering outside, listening to the sounds of my family in the house below, I think I know which model I choose. Put the gun to your head, Harris, and say it: "Yes. I think so. I don't know. No. I hope so. Yes."'

Bible references: Matthew 4:18-22; 9:9; 19:27; 28:19-20; Mark 1:16-20; 2:14; 10:28; Luke 5:2-11, 27-8; 18:28; John 20:29; Acts 1:8; Hebrews 11:1.

Source: Adapted from the *Daily Telegraph*, 25 May 1996. © Telegraph Group Ltd, London 1996.

16. Conversion: Festo Kivengere's story

(Atonement, Conversion, The Cross, Evangelism, Forgiveness, Friendship, Liberation, Priorities, Repentance, Salvation, Testimony, Time, Witness)

It was Sunday 5 October. The young Ugandan schoolteacher was in a bad mood. He had stormed out of church earlier that day, enraged by the Christian message that was being preached, and had spent the rest of the day drinking. Then a friend rode up to him on a bicycle, and called out, 'When I was in church today, something happened to me. God has forgiven me the wrongs I have done. Jesus has become my Saviour!' Apologising for various wrongs he had done, the friend rode off.

It was like a thunderclap for the schoolteacher. How could his friend betray him in this way, changing his mind about Jesus Christ? It was too much! Years later, he told how this encounter on the road had been a crucial turning-point. 'I made for my room. I was kneeling, seeking forgiveness, seeking restoration. I began to cry to God, and my eyes were opened to his love on the cross. I realised that the death of Christ was because of me. Then it was as if the Lord said, "This is also how much I love *you*." I felt a tremendous liberation. I had been running away from God's love, and now this freedom! I jumped to my feet. I remember saying, "Lord, give me permission for one more week... just one more week to live, and I will tell everyone I meet about this!"'

Festo Kivengere was as good as his word. He rushed outside and shouted to a woman who was passing by, 'Stop! Stop! Jesus Christ has come my way today!' The woman assumed he was drunk, and looked the other way. But Festo Kivengere went on to be greatly used by God as an evangelist across Africa, and as a highly–respected and influential leader of the church in Uganda.

Bible references: Isaiah 53:4-6; Luke 23:43; John 3:16-17; Acts 2:13-15; 9:1-19; 22:6-21; 26:12-20; Romans 4:25-5:2; Hebrews 9:28; 1 Peter 2:24-5.

Source: Adapted from Richard Bewes, *The Church Overcomes* (Mowbray, 1984), pp 8-9.

17. Evangelism

(Belief, Conversion, Death, Priorities, Salvation, Testimony, Witness)

When the *Titanic* went down on 15 April 1912, some 1,595 people perished in the icy waters of the North Atlantic. Many more could have been rescued, but there were only enough lifeboats for half the number of people aboard. One of those who was unable to find a place in a lifeboat was a Glasgow preacher, John Harper. As he clung to a piece of wreckage in the tossing sea, he shared the good news of the love of God with another passenger, a fellow Scotsman, who was clinging to a spar not far away. Eventually the preacher could hold on no longer, and met his death in the bitterly cold water. But the Scotsman survived to tell the tale of how, as he himself put it later, 'There, alone in the night and with two miles of water under me, I believed. I am John Harper's last convert.'

Bible references: Matthew 28:19-20; Acts 1:8; 27:13-44; Romans 1:16; 1 Corinthians 9:16; 2 Corinthians 11:25.

Source: Adapted from Richard Bewes, *The Church Overcomes* (Mowbray, 1984), p 44.

18. Evangelism

(Commitment,   Discipleship,   Gospel,   Mission,   Sacrifice, Witness)

In the western world we have so many hang-ups about sharing our faith with others. We read books, go on courses, and still find ourselves tongue-tied with embarrassment. The church in Nepal saw tremendous growth in the 1990s, and a British teacher in Pakistan asked a colleague who had been over there what the secret of the Nepalis' success was. 'They've got a very simple technique,' his friend replied. 'They tell others about Jesus.'

At the same time, Western Christians can often fail to appreciate the cost of following Christ in other parts of the world. The Indonesian evangelist Octavianus, preaching to Muslims in southern Thailand, put it plainly. 'Come to Christ!' he appealed. 'It may cost you your life, but come all the same.'

Bible references: Matthew 10:34-9; 16:24-7; 28:19-20; Mark 8:34-8; Luke 9:23-6; John 12:23-6; Acts 1:8; Romans 1:16; 2 Timothy 1:8-9, 12.

Source: David Fletcher of the Church Missionary Society; Dick Dowsett of the Overseas Missionary Fellowship.

19. Evangelism

(Christianity,   Conversion,   Criticism,   Crusades,   History, Missionaries, Opposition, Vikings, Violence)

Looking back at some of the things that our forebears did in the name of Christ can make us cringe with embarrassment. In the year 997, King Olaf Tryggvason of Norway sent a Saxon priest named Thangbrand to preach the gospel in Iceland, which was still pagan. Thangbrand's methods could be called 'muscular Christianity', as this extract from the medieval *Njal's Saga* shows.

'The following spring Thangbrand set out to preach Christianity, but when they came to Staffel, they found a man living there named Thorkell. He spoke out against the faith, and challenged Thangbrand to single combat. Then Thangbrand bore a crucifix before his shield, and the outcome of the battle was that Thangbrand won the day and killed Thorkell. Then they went on to Hornfirth and stayed with Hilldir the Old, and he and all his household accepted the new faith.

'They then travelled to Dyrholms and held a meeting there to preach the faith, and Ingialld became a Christian. Going on to Fleetlithe they preached the faith there, too, but Weatherlid the Poet and his son Ari spoke out against the faith, and for that they slew Weatherlid.'

Bible references: 2 Kings 1:1-15; 2:23-4; Matthew 26:51-2; Mark 14:47; Luke 9:52-6; 22:49-50; John 18:10-11.

Source: Adapted from Sir George Webbe Dasent, *The Story of Burnt Njal* (Everyman, 1911), pp 177-8.

20. Forgiveness

(Conversion, Crime, Freedom, Grace, Guilt, Pardon, Prison, Repentance, Salvation, Sin, Testimony)

As a young man, Bob Sheffield was a professional hockey

player in Canada. He was a tough guy and often got into fights, and after one bar-room brawl he ended up spending the night in jail. But then Bob became a Christian, and his life-style and behaviour changed. He started to work in Christian ministry for the Navigators, and was asked to go on tempo-rary assignment for them in the United States. The problem arose when Bob applied for landed immigrant status: because he had a criminal record, this was automatically denied.

Although Bob could still get a temporary visa, he realised that his past would continue to be a problem whenever he was asked to work abroad. So he applied for a royal pardon, and after a while, to his delight, the request was granted. This meant that if ever he was asked by anyone whether he had a criminal record, he could sincerely and truthfully answer 'No'. If ever a police department should look him up on their computer files, they would find 'No record' against his name. That is what it means to be pardoned.

Bible references: Exodus 34:6-7; Nehemiah 9:17; Psalm 51; 103; Isaiah 1:18; 55:6-7; 1 Corinthians 6:9-11; 2 Corinthians 5:17-21; Ephesians 2:1-10; Colossians 2:13-15; 1 Peter 2:24-25.

Source: Adapted from Tom Eisenman, *Temptations Men Face* (Kingsway, 1991), pp 21-2.

21. Old age

(Alpha, Conversion, Discipleship, Evangelism, Faith, Gospel, Witness)

Winifred Brown became a Christian at the age of sixty-eight, and always tried to share her faith with her elderly neighbours in the other mobile homes on the caravan park where she lived. She found that doing an Alpha course gave her confidence a tremendous boost.

'My sister tells everyone, "Our Win's gone all funny and religious." But I don't mind. I'm much more sure in my faith now. We had the Jehovah's Witnesses round yesterday and I held my ground with them, which I wouldn't have done before. But I'd like to go through Alpha all over again, because there's still a lot more to learn, even at my age!'

Bible references: Luke 2:25-38; Romans 1:16; Colossians 4:5-6; 2 Timothy 1:8-9, 12; 1 Peter 3:15-16.

Source: Adapted from *Alpha News*, September 1994.

22. Peace

(Conversion, Gospel, Love, Murder, Prison, Terrorism, Violence)

If proof were ever needed that the gospel of peace and the love of Christ can overcome the deepest divisions within human society, it is surely provided by this brief wedding announcement from 1993:

On Thursday at Maghaberry jail in County Antrim, Anne Moore, the Republican terrorist serving life for the murder of eleven soldiers and six civilians in the 1982 bombing in Ballykelly, plans to marry Bobby Corry, another terrorist jailed for life for murder, but in the Unionist interest. Both Moore and Corry have become born-again Christians and renounced violence.

Bible references: 1 Corinthians 6:9-11; 12:13; 2 Corinthians 5:17-21; Galatians 3:26-8; Ephesians 2:1-10, 13-17; Colossians 2:13-15; 3:11; 1 Peter 2:24-5.

Source: the *Daily Telegraph*, 20 March 1993.

23. Witness: Chen's story

(Conversion, Evangelism, Faith, Faithfulness, Fear, Guidance, Love, Persecution, Prison, Suffering, Testimony, Torture)

Chen is a Chinese Christian woman who was imprisoned and tortured for her faith by old-style Communists. After one particularly brutal session she was thrown into a cell with two hardened criminals. These women apparently hated Chen, and completely ignored her, but Chen was filled with compassion for her cell mates. All night long they kept her awake with their wailing and groaning, and Chen discovered that they were both deeply afraid of dying.

Chen prayed for the women, and felt the Holy Spirit was telling her to show them kindness in practical ways. So she decided to fast, and gave her meagre rations to the two other women. They were utterly perplexed by this, but gobbled the food down quickly in case Chen changed her mind. Gradually the atmosphere in the cell changed. Never having been shown kindness, the two convicts were deeply touched by the love Chen showed them. And then, and only then, she started telling them about the love of Christ. It wasn't long before they asked how they, too, could know Jesus for themselves.

The two women made their commitment to Christ kneeling in their prison cell, knowing that as believers their treatment would be even worse. They might even face death – but this was now a prospect they no longer dreaded. Yet in an ironic twist, the transformation in their behaviour persuaded the prison authorities to release them early! Today both women are tireless in their efforts to lead other criminals to Christ.

Bible references: Exodus 4:12; Matthew 5:11-12; 10:17-25; 24:9; Mark 13:9-13; Luke 12:11-12; 21:12-19; John 15:18-21; Acts 16:23-34.

Source: Adapted from Michael Apichella, 'The Holy Spirit in China', *Renewal*, March 1996.

24. Witness

(Conversion, Evangelism, Faith, Prayer, Testimony, Work)

A Christian farmer with a sick cow had to call out the vet to have a look at it. The vet happened to be an atheist. After he had finished the treatment, the farmer said, 'Do you mind if we pray for the cow now?' Although the vet thought this was a waste of time, the farmer was paying for him to be there, so he couldn't really say no. The farmer prayed, and the vet went on his way. The cow later died, but the vet was deeply impressed by the farmer's faith. Several years later, when he finally became a Christian, he said that the farmer's prayer had been the turning point.

Bible references: Matthew 5:13-16; Mark 4:21; Luke 8:16; Colossians 3:23-4; 1 Peter 3:1, 15-16.

Source: *A Man's Life* (CPAS) p 21.

THE BIBLE

25. Acts of the Apostles

(Animals, Apocrypha, Early Church, Insects, Miracles, Humour)

There were many different 'Acts' of the various apostles written in the first centuries of the Christian church, but as this extract from the third-century *Acts of John* reveals, they were very different from Luke's rather more sober account.

We arrived at a lonely inn, and while we were trying to find a bed for John we noticed a curious thing. There was one unoccupied and unmade bed, so we spread the cloaks which we were wearing over it, and begged him to lie down on it, while all the rest of us slept on the floor.

But when John lay down he was troubled by the bugs. They became more and more troublesome to him, and it was already midnight when he said to them in the hearing of us all, 'I order you, bugs, to behave yourselves one and all. You must leave your home for tonight and be quiet in one place, and keep your distance from the servants of

God.' And while we laughed and went on talking, John went to sleep, but we talked quietly and, thanks to him, were not disturbed.

Now as day was breaking, I got up first, and Verus and Andronicus with me, and we saw by the door of the room which we had taken an enormous mass of bugs. We were astounded at their great number. All the brethren woke up because of them, but John went on sleeping. When he woke up, we explained to him what we had seen. He sat up in bed, looked at the bugs and said, 'Since you have behaved yourselves and listened to my correction, you may go back to your own place.' When he had said this, and had got up from the bed, the bugs came running from the door towards the bed, climbed up its legs, and disappeared into the joints.

Bible references: Genesis 1:26-8; 9:2; Psalm 8:6-8; 115:16.

Source: Quoted in Jerome Murphy O'Connor, *Archaeology in the World of Herod, Jesus and Paul* (Biblical Archaeology Society, 1990), p 276.

26. Amazing discoveries

(Archaeology, Heaven, Holy Communion, Journalism, Media, Newspapers, Outer space, Humour)

An American tabloid newspaper, the *Weekly World News*, made two remarkable claims in a single issue, that of 30 April 1996: the discovery of an original, handwritten invitation to the Last Supper, and the existence of a photograph of heaven!

In the first story ('Invitation to Last Supper Found in Holy Land'), the newspaper reported that a 'well-worn paper' written in Hebrew had been uncovered in Bethany. It purportedly reads: 'Come, partake at a supper of great importance.... We will experience a final gathering in the room where we have met many times before.' The tabloid quoted the supposed finder of the scrap of paper, said to be a French archaeologist named Guy Millet, as saying, 'Of course, there is a possibility that Jesus actually wrote the invitations.'

As if this did not offer sufficient excitement, the newspaper offered another scoop elsewhere in the same edition, under the headline: 'Heaven Photographed by Hubble Telescope.' The subheading helpfully added: '"We found where God lives," says scientist!' The article stated that 'the pictures clearly show a vast white city floating eerily in the blackness of space', and quoted 'author and researcher' Marcia Masson as saying that NASA scientists at first 'couldn't believe their eyes. After checking and rechecking the data, they concluded that the images were authentic.... The only logical explanation was that the city was inhabited by the souls of the dead.' Eager to help its readers locate heaven for themselves, the paper also included a map showing its location beyond the edge of the universe.

Bible references: Matthew 26:17-30; Mark 14:12-26; Luke 22:7-20; 1 Corinthians 11:23-5; Hebrews 11:6; 12:22-3; 13:14; Revelation 21; 22.

Source: Adapted from *Biblical Archaeology Review*, July/August 1996.

27. A comedy of errors

*(Commandments,   Mistakes,   Misunderstanding,   New
Testament, Old Testament, Students, Teachers, Humour)*

What the teacher tries to teach is, as many of us know all too
well, not always the same as what the student hears, still less
remembers. The following survey of Biblical history consists
of genuine extracts from student essays about the Scriptures.

The Bible is full of interesting caricatures.

In the first book of the Bible, Guinesses, Adam and Eve
were created from an apple tree.

The first commandment was when Eve told Adam to eat
the apple.

One of their children, Cain, once asked, 'Am I my brother's
son?'

Noah's wife was called Joan of Ark.

God asked Abraham to sacrifice Isaac on Mount
Montezuma.

Jacob, son of Isaac, stole his brother's birth mark.

Jacob was a patriarch who brought up his twelve sons to be
patriarchs, but they did not take to it.

One of Jacob's sons, Joseph, gave refuse to the Israelites.

Pharaoh forced the Hebrew slaves to make bread without
straw.

Moses led them to the Red Sea, where they made
unleavened bread, which is bread made without any
ingredients.

Afterwards, Moses went up on Mount Cyanide to get the
Ten Commandments.

One commandment is not to admit adultery.

Another is: Do not convert your neighbour's wife.

And another: Humour thy father and thy mother.

David was a Hebrew king skilled at playing the liar.

He fought with the Philatelists, a race of people who lived in Biblical times.

Solomon, one of David's sons, had 500 wives and 500 porcupines.

When Mary heard she was to be the mother of Jesus, she went off and sang the Magna Carta.

Jesus mixed with tax collectors and ministers who were protestants.

The tenth leopard when he saw that he had lost his spots went back to say thank you.

Jesus rowed into Jerusalem on a donkey.

Salome was a woman who danced naked in front of Harrods.

Bible references: Genesis 2; 3; 4:9; 6-8; 22; 25:29-34; 35:23-6; 42-5; 46:8-25; Exodus 5:6-21; 14; 19-20; 20:12, 14, 17; Deuteronomy 5:16, 18, 21; 1 Samuel 16:15-18; 1 Kings 11:3; Matthew 14:6; 21:1-9; Mark 6:22; 11:1-10; Luke 2:46-55; 17:11-19; 19:29-38.

Source: Combined from Richard Lederer, 'The World According to Student Bloopers'; *Word in Action,* 1992; *Church of England Newspaper,* May 1996.

28. Gospels

(Apocrypha, Childhood, Jesus, Miracles)

Many alternative accounts of the life of Jesus circulated in the early centuries of the Christian church, among them the so-called *Infancy Gospel of Thomas* (not to be confused with the Gnostic *Gospel of Thomas*). It was especially popular in the eastern church and was apparently known to Muhammad, to judge by its influence on the Qur'an. Only one story in the *Infancy Gospel* has any relationship with the Bible, the account of the twelve-year-old Jesus in the Temple. The rest is pure fantasy, an imaginative portrait of what a divine child might be like.

It begins with the young Jesus making clay birds on the Sabbath, then clapping his hands to make them fly away. The boy carries water home in his clothing when his pitcher is broken, causes a miraculous crop of corn to grow, and stretches some wood to solve a carpentry problem faced by Joseph. There are also various stories about Jesus' playmates. In one of them a boy named Zeno falls to his death from the upper storey of a house, and when Jesus is accused by Zeno's parents of causing the accident, he jumps down from the roof and brings Zeno back to life so that he can tell his parents that this wasn't true! On another occasion, Jesus curses the son of Annas for spoiling his game, causing the lad to wither on the spot; on yet another he curses a boy who bumps into him, whereupon the boy drops dead, and those who remonstrate with Jesus are struck blind. All this leads Joseph to grumble to Mary, 'Don't let him go outside the door, for all those who provoke him end up dead'!

Bible references: Matthew 21:18-20; Mark 11:12-14; 20-21; Luke 2:41-52.

Source: R. T. France, *The Evidence for Jesus* (Hodder and Stoughton, 1986), pp 73-4; R. H. Mounce, *Matthew* (Hendrickson, 1991), p 21.

29. Gospels

(Books, Courage, Early Church, Martyrdom, Persecution, Sacrifice, Suffering, Testimony, Witness)

On 17 July 180, seven men and five women stood trial in Carthage in North Africa. Boldly confessing their faith in Jesus Christ, despite the threat of execution, they were condemned to die by the sword.

During the trial, they were asked by the governor, 'What do you have there in your bag?' 'Books,' replied one of the twelve, 'and letters of Paul, a good man.'

The books in question were almost certainly Gospels, and perhaps some of the books of the Old Testament as well. In the view of these early Christians, these were books worth dying for.

Bible references: Matthew 10:17-22, 39; 16:24-7; Mark 8:34-8; 13:9-13; Luke 9:23-6; 12:11-12; 21:12-19; John 12:24-6; 15:18-21; Acts 4:18-20; Romans 1:16; 2 Timothy 1:8-9.

Source: Adapted from Stephen Travis, in *Floodtide*, July-August 1995.

30. Jonah

(Children, Fish, Freedom, Mistakes, Humour)

The Old Testament prophet Jonah was swallowed by a large fish, yet survived unscathed to tell the tale. In 1995, a two-year-old girl from Bedworth in Warwickshire gave the family's pet goldfish a taste of what it must have been like for poor Jonah. Joanne Hackleton, who reportedly loves fish fingers, swallowed the fish while nobody was watching. The first her parents knew of it was when she went to her mother saying, 'Fish gone, fish gone,' and they noticed that the goldfish bowl was empty. But thankfully, that was not the end of the story. Twenty minutes and a glass of salt water later, the goldfish popped out alive, and returned to the tranquillity of its tank.

Bible references: Jonah 1:17-2:10; Matthew 12:39-40; Luke 11:29-30.

Source: Adapted from the *Daily Telegraph*, 8 April 1995.

31. Misprints

(Adultery, Beatitudes, Commandments, God, Kingdom of God, Mistakes, Sin, Humour)

Printing a book as long as the Bible meant that there was always the possibility of misprints, some of which proved very costly to the printers concerned.

● The 'Wicked Bible' of 1631 is perhaps the most notorious. The seventh commandment read: 'Thou shalt commit adultery', an omission which led to the King's printers, Barker and Lucas of Blackfriars, being fined £3000 and consequently going out of business.

● Another Bible of just three years later, 1634, rendered Psalm 14:1: 'The fool hath said in his heart, "There is a God"'; an error for which the printers were again fined the enormous sum of £3000.

● Not much better was the 'Unrighteous Bible' of 1653, in which 1 Corinthians 6:9 read: 'Know ye that the unrighteous shall inherit the kingdom of God?'

● Jesus' words in Mark 7:27, 'Let the children first be filled', were unfortunately mangled in a Bible of 1795, reading instead: 'Let the children first be killed'!

● In a version of 1562, Matthew 5:9 read: 'Blessed are the placemakers'.

Bible references: Exodus 20:14; Deuteronomy 5:18; Psalm 14:1; Matthew 5:9; Mark 7:27; 1 Corinthians 6:9.

Source: Quoted in Russell Ash and Brian Lake, *Bizarre Books* (Macmillan, 1985), pp 145-8.

32. Obedience

(Commandments, Discipleship, Lifestyle, Understanding, Humour)

Someone once said to the American humorist Will Rogers, 'The Bible troubles me because there are parts of it I just don't understand.' Quick as a flash Rogers replied, 'It troubles me because there are parts of it that I do understand!'

Bible references: Luke 16:29-31; John 5:39-40, 45-7; 2 Peter 3:16.

Source: Quoted in James Ryle, *Hippo in the Garden* (Highland, 1992), p 73.

33. Revelation

(Apocalypse, Bible study, Health, Hypochondriacs, Humour)

Too much study of the book of Revelation has always had its dangers, as this report reveals:

> Peter Jurieu, who was formerly famous for his labours in writing books of controversy, and expounding the Apocalypse, so disorder'd his brain, that though he thought like a man in other respects, he was firmly persuaded that the seven fits of cholic with which he was tormented, had been occasioned by a constant fight between seven horsemen that were shut up in his bowels.

Bible references: Ecclesiastes 12:12; Zechariah 1:8; 6:2; Revelation 6:1-8.

Source: Samuel Tissot, *An Essay on Diseases Incidental to Literary and Sedentary Persons*, quoted in Russell Ash and Brian Lake, *Bizarre Books* (Macmillan, 1985), p 93.

34. Translation

(History, Language, Literature, Humour)

In the eighteenth century a man named Edward Harwood decided to produce a proper literary translation of the Scriptures in the 'refined and polished' language of his own day. This is his version of Matthew 6:28-9:

> Survey with attention the lilies of the field, and learn from them how unbecoming it is for rational creatures to cherish

a solicitous passion for gaiety and dress – for they sustain no labour, they employ no cares to adorn themselves, and yet are clothed with such inimitable beauty as the richest monarch in the richest dress never equalled.

Bible references: Matthew 6:28-9.

Source: Quoted in review of David Norton, *A History of the Bible as Literature,* vol. 2, in *The Expository Times,* March 1994, p 162.

35. The twelve apostles

(Business, Gifts, Gospels, Jesus, Management, Talents, Work, Humour)

To: Jesus, son of Joseph, carpenter's shop, Nazareth.
From: Jordan Management Consultants, Jerusalem.

It is our opinion that the twelve men you have picked to manage your new organisation lack the background, educational and vocational aptitude for the type of enterprise you are undertaking. They do not have the team concept.

Simon Peter is emotionally unstable and given to fits of temper. Andrew has no qualities of leadership. The two brothers James and John place personal interest above company loyalty. Thomas demonstrates a questioning attitude that would tend to undermine morale.

We feel it is our duty to tell you that Matthew has been blacklisted by the Greater Jerusalem Better Business Bureau.

James, the son of Alphaeus, and Thaddeus have racial leanings and both registered high on the manic-depressive scale.

One of the candidates, however, shows great potential. He is a man of ability and resourcefulness, has a keen business mind and contacts in high places. He is highly motivated and ambitious. We recommend Judas Iscariot as your controller and right-hand man.

We wish you every success in your new venture.

Bible references: Matthew 10:2-4; 16:22; 26:14-16; 26:69-75; Mark 3:16-19; Luke 6:14-16; 9:52-6; John 1:40-2; 13:6-9, 29; 18:10; 20:24-8; Acts 1:13.

Source: Quoted in *Readers' Digest* 1990.

36. The word of God

(Bible study, Discipleship, Eternity, Faith, Hope, Hostages, Life, Lifestyle, Prison, Purpose)

Emanuel Christen and Elio Erriquez were Swiss Red Cross workers who were taken hostage by Lebanese militants in 1989. Despite spending 312 days locked in a small room, their faith helped bring them through the ordeal, as Emanuel Christen explained after their release.

From a spiritual angle the time I spent in captivity was a great gain. At thirty-three years old I believe I have just begun to understand what living the Christian life really means.

One day, one of our jailers who used to give us bits of reading material from time to time left a cardboard box with various oddments in it. Rummaging around among the loose sheets we found what we recognised to be part of a Bible in English, but it was in old English and partially burned. It lacked a good deal of the Old Testament, but the New Testament was complete. What incredible joy we felt!

With the help of an English-French dictionary, which stopped at the letter N, we were able to read the Bible every day and reflect on it, and because of this we began to change our attitude towards our jailers. It is wonderful to experience an about-turn in your feelings, and as we read the Bible we felt God working in our lives, and we responded to the message of the Bible. We were in the habit of referring to our jailers by nasty and abusive names. Now we decided to give them new, encouraging names – and this was no minor detail for us, shut up for weeks on end in that prison, with nothing to do.

Everything about us began to change because of that Bible. No one in captivity can hold out without hope, and the Bible is full of hope – hope of what is not seen, hope in the reality of God. I began to understand that our temporary reality, our being hostages, was only a shadow of our true life, eternal life, and I knew that God had allowed us to be taken hostage so that we might understand this. Now that I am free, my aim is to discover what path God has chosen for me, and to follow it.

Bible references: Isaiah 55:10-11; Romans 8:18-25; 1 Corinthians 13:12; 2 Corinthians 4:16-18; 5:6-9; Colossians 1:4-6; 2 Timothy 3:15-17; Hebrews 4:12; 11:1.

Source: *Word in Action,* 1992.

37. The word of God

(Conversion,   Discipleship,   Lifestyle,   Missionaries, Obedience, War)

When American troops captured the island of Okinawa towards the end of the Second World War, they found it in a state of moral and social collapse. As they gradually advanced through the island, they came to the village of Shimbakuku. There they were greeted by two men, one of them carrying a Bible. The GIs suspected a trap, and entered the village cautiously, but to their amazement they found everything neat and tidy, the fields tilled and fertile, and the whole village a model of order and hygiene, in total contrast to the squalor and chaos which reigned everywhere else. One of the old men who had welcomed them explained the reason to them.

Some thirty years earlier, an American missionary had stopped off in Shimbakuku on his way to Japan. He didn't stay long, and just two people became Christians – the two old men. He taught them a few hymns and prayers, and left them a Japanese translation of the Bible, urging them to model their lives on it. The two men had no other Christian teaching or fellowship, but by basing their lives on what they read in the Bible they transformed their community. When the American soldiers arrived, they found no jail, no brothel, no drunkenness and no divorce. Shimbakuku was an oasis of love and purity in a swamp of degradation and despair.

The war correspondent who first brought the story to light, a man named Clarence Hall, quoted his dumbfounded driver: 'So this is what comes out of only a Bible and a couple of old men who want to live like Jesus! Maybe we're using the wrong kind of weapons to change the world.'

Bible references: Psalm 19:7-11; 119; Isaiah 55:10-11; John

5:39; 1 Thessalonians 2:13; 2 Timothy 3:15-17; Hebrews 4:12.

Source: Adapted from James A. Feehan, *Preaching in Stories* (The Mercier Press, 1989), pp 26-7.

PRAYER

38. Answers to prayer

(Health, Life, Poverty, Power, Sickness, Strength, Weakness, Wealth)

An otherwise unknown Confederate soldier wrote this prayer during the American civil war:

I asked God for strength that I might achieve,
I was made weak, that I might learn humbly to obey.
I asked for health, that I might do greater things,
I was given infirmity, that I might do better things.
I asked for riches, that I might be happy,
I was given poverty, that I might be wise.
I asked for power, that I might have the praise of men,
I was given weakness, that I might feel the need of God.
I asked for all things, that I might enjoy life,
I was given life, that I might enjoy all things.
I got nothing that I asked for,
but everything I hoped for.
Almost, despite myself, my unspoken prayers were
    answered.

I among all men most richly blessed.

Bible references: Proverbs 30:7-9; Matthew 5:3-12; 1 Corinthians 1:17-31; 2 Corinthians 4:7-12; 6:4-10; 12:7-10; Philippians 4:11-13.

Source: Quoted in Russ Parker, *Free to Fail* (Triangle, 1992), pp 120-1.

39. Busyness

(God, Presence of God, Time, Work, War)

In the rush and bustle of so much of modern life, there are surely many people who would readily echo Sir Jacob Astley's prayer before the Civil War battle of Edgehill, on 23 October 1642: 'O Lord, thou knowest how busy I must be this day. If I forget thee, do not thou forget me.'

Bible references: Exodus 33:15-16; Isaiah 49:14-16.

Source: Quoted in Christopher Hibbert, *Cavaliers and Roundheads* (HarperCollins, 1993), p 79.

40. Commitment

(Church, Faithfulness, Growth, Old age, Retirement)

'Every morning at five o'clock my church meets for prayer.
   'It started in a very interesting way: an old lady, about

eighty-five years old, came to one of the pastors of the church and said, "Pastor, can we have a little room here in the church to pray every morning at five o'clock? I feel that God wants me to spend the rest of my life in prayer and I have a small prayer group who want to meet every morning for those who are going to work. We are old ladies, we are retired, and we want to give those morning hours to God for prayer."

'So the pastor said, "Yes, of course, you can have a room here." And that lady came with five other ladies and they started to pray.

'Two days later the pastor was very curious about what was happening there, so he went to see. As soon as he stepped into that room, he felt that he should stay there. After the pastor joined the prayer group, other people heard, and the group started to grow.

'The group grew to twenty, thirty, forty. There was no more room in that office for them, so they moved. Now, every morning we have 400 to 500 people meeting to pray.'

Bible references: Exodus 24:4; 32:6; Judges 21:4; 1 Samuel 1:19; 2 Chronicles 29:20; Job 1:5; Mark 1:35.

Source: Pastor Paul Negrut, head of Romanian Evangelical Alliance, in *Renewal*, 1993.

41. Confession

(Church, Excuses, Guilt, Liturgical reform, Liturgy, Modern Life, Sin, Humour)

In 1976, a major Protestant denomination narrowly defeated an attempt to destigmatize the Prayer of Confession by removing from it all guilt or guilt-oriented references: 'Lord, we approach Thy Throne of Grace, having committed acts which, we do heartily acknowledge, must be very difficult for Thee to understand. Nevertheless, we do beseech Thee to postpone judgement and to give Thy faithful servants the benefit of the doubt until such time as we are able to answer all Thy questions fully and clear our reputations in Heaven.'

Bible references: Leviticus 26:40-2; 1 Samuel 7:6; Ezra 10:11; Nehemiah 1:6-7; 9:1-3; Psalm 51; Isaiah 59:12-13; Daniel 9:4-6; James 5:16; 1 John 1:9.

Source: Garrison Keillor, *We are Still Married* (Faber and Faber, 1989), p 24.

42. Contemplation

(Listening, Peace, Presence of God, Silence)

It is like the experience of two lovers holding hands. If asked, what did you say to each other? Nothing. What did you do? Again, nothing. What then happened? Everything! So likewise in contemplative prayer, the heart is mightily affected in the presence of God, yet the experience is wordless.

Bible references: Psalm 131.

Source: James Houston, *The Transforming Friendship* (Lion, 1989), p 255.

43. Forgiveness

(Bitterness, Blame, Business, Liberation, Lord's Prayer, Love, Power of God, Testimony, Work)

After setting up his own company, Ian Gordon had suffered the indignity of being asked to resign by the Board. The man who had forced his resignation, and in his eyes the villain of the piece, was one Henry Cavendish. But redundancy proved to have a silver lining: in his despair, Ian came to a living faith in Christ. He threw himself into the Christian life enthusiastically. One day, he was saying the Lord's Prayer when God spoke to him with a challenge.

I came to the line, 'Forgive us our trespasses as we forgive those who trespass against us,' when I felt the Lord interrupt me with a question. 'Do you really know what you're asking? You want me to forgive you, but I can't truly forgive you until you first forgive Henry.'

I stopped dead in my tracks. I hadn't consciously thought about Henry for some time... but now here I was, confronted with my own lack of forgiveness. I felt no inclination whatsoever to forgive the man whom I blamed for my present situation, and I told the Lord this. 'I've lost everything,' I said, 'my company, my work, my money, and I'm about to lose this house. I *can't* forgive him.' Even as I spoke, I knew that I was totally wrong in my thinking; I hardly had the right to ask God for forgiveness when I was so obdurate about Henry, but try as I might, I could not summon up one ounce of even the most lukewarm feelings. Then something came into my mind that I had read recently in one of the Christian books that I was devouring daily: 'When you find it impossible to do something, ask the Lord to do it through you; when you can't do something in your own strength, do it in his.' It was like light dawning....

I prayed from my heart for God to let his forgiveness flow through me to the man who, in my mind, had wronged me. As I prayed, I felt the love of God pass through me like a current of warm air from the top of my head to the soles of my feet, and I knew that God was taking away all the wrong feelings that I had towards Henry. The release was incredible. I hadn't realised it, but the hurt I was carrying inside had been like a heavy stone, and now it had been lifted from me. I could not believe how light and carefree I now felt. I began to pray for the man whom not so very long ago I had wanted to destroy, and felt a love for him where before there had been hatred.

Bible references: Matthew 6:12, 14-15; 18:21-35; Mark 11:25; Luke 6:27-37; 11:4; 17:3-4; John 20:23; Ephesians 4:32; Colossians 3:13.

Source: Ian Gordon, *The Craft and the Cross* (Kingsway, 1989), pp 141-2.

44. Grace before meals

(Animals, Answers to prayer, Conversion, Fear, Miracles, Humour)

A man was being chased by a lion, and every time he looked back he could see that the lion was gaining on him. So in desperation he cried out, 'Lord, make this lion a Christian!' To his utter amazement, the lion slowed down, and then stopped altogether. It sat down, folded its paws and closed its eyes, and began moving its lips as if in prayer. The astonished man came closer to hear what it was that the lion was praying, and was just in time to hear it say, 'For what we are about to receive, may the Lord make us truly thankful.'

Source: Adapted from Gordon and Gail Macdonald, *Till the Heart be Touched* (Highland Books, 1992), p 140.

45. Guidance

(Hearing God, Listening, Voice of God, Work)

Linda Anderson was sitting in her car at some traffic lights in Watford when she distinctly, but quite unexpectedly, heard God say to her, 'I want you to be a schools' worker.' Linda had been praying about what she should do when her youngest daughter started school, but she hadn't even considered the possibility of Christian schools' work. The next day she spoke to her minister. He told her that the previous day he had been at a ministers' fraternal. As it happened, they had been discussing the situation in local schools, and had decided that they needed to appoint another Christian worker. The meeting had been taking place at the very time Linda was sitting waiting for the lights to change.

Bible references: Exodus 3:4; 1 Samuel 3:1-18; Psalm 32:8; Isaiah 30:21; Jeremiah 1:4-10; Amos 7:14-15; John 10:3-5; Acts 9:4; 10:13-15.

Source: Adapted from Scripture Union, *Outreach,* Spring 1994.

46. Hearing God

(Presence of God, Voice of God, Humour)

A burglar broke into a house one night, and had gone into the sitting room when a voice echoed out of the darkness, 'I'm watching you, and Jesus is watching you.' The startled burglar flashed his torch round the room, but couldn't see anybody. Then the voice spoke again, 'I'm watching you, and Jesus is watching you.' Throwing caution to the winds, the burglar found the light switch, and turned the light on. There in the corner of the room was a parrot in a cage, and as the light went on he said his piece again, 'I'm watching you, and Jesus is watching you.' The burglar went up to the cage and said, 'You didn't half give me a fright! What's your name, then?' 'Fred,' the parrot answered. 'Fred?' repeated the burglar, 'That's a stupid name for a parrot!' 'Maybe,' said the parrot, 'but then Jesus is a stupid name for a Rottweiler.'

Source: Russell Bowman-Eadie, Wells 1995.

47. Intercession

(Answers to prayer, Death, Health, Life, Medicine, Royalty, Science)

In 1995 an experiment was conducted in San Francisco regarding the efficacy of intercessory prayer. Some 200 patients who were admitted to the State General Hospital following a heart attack were assigned to a group of Christians who regularly prayed for their recovery, while another 200 acted as a control group, receiving identical medical treatment, but without the benefit of prayer. The result was that significantly fewer of those being prayed for died or saw their condition worsen through a stroke or further heart attack while in hospital. Dr Randolph Byrd, who organised the study, commented that 'intercessory prayer has a beneficial therapeutic effect'.

This stands in marked contrast to the conclusions of the great Victorian scientist Francis Galton. He argued that nobody in England was prayed for more frequently than the royal family, so that if intercessory prayer really worked, they should have enjoyed significantly better health and longer lives than the general population. But a table of their life expectancy which he compiled showed that precisely the reverse was true. Of course, we cannot tell how fervent or sincere were the prayers which were made on their behalf!

Bible references: James 5:14-16.

Source: Adapted from the *Daily Telegraph*, 30 March 1995.

48. The Lord's Prayer

(Answers to prayer, Belief, Confession, God, Lottery, Religion, Shallow prayer, Sin, Unbelief)

Trevor Dearing once wrote: 'The shallowest prayer of which I have ever heard is that of a man who wrote the Lord's Prayer out on a piece of card and pinned it above his bed. Every night before he went to sleep he pointed to it and said, "That's my prayer, Lord!" and then dozed off.'

The National Lottery has engendered equally mindless petitions. The BBC in its weekly lottery draw has actually referred to 'The Lottery Prayer' – 'Lord, I know I'm a sinner, but make me a winner'. That some people really do think like this was revealed when a Mormon knocked on yet another door and was told by the woman who answered: 'I know there's no God, because I pray every Friday and I still haven't won the lottery.'

Bible references: Matthew 6:7-13; Luke 11:2-4; James 4:3; 1 John 5:14.

Source: *Renewal*, February 1992; BBC TV, June 1996.

49. Perseverance

(Church and state, Faithfulness, Intercession, Martyrdom, Nazism, Persecution, Prison, Suffering, War)

On 1 July 1937, the Gestapo arrested Pastor Martin Niemöller, one of the leaders of the Confessing Church, which opposed the Nazi regime. The men arrived at 8.30 am, telling Niemöller that he was to go with them for questioning. By this time he was used to such interrogation sessions, and he went expecting to be back with his family by nightfall. But this time was different. The pastor was put in a cell, and although he waited and waited to be called for questioning, the summons never came. He was to remain a prisoner of the Nazis for the next eight years.

During this time the Church never forgot him. In the little mission church of St Anne's, which was attached to his own parish church, services of intercession were held for him from the day of his arrest until the end of the war, at first twice a week, and then daily. The meetings were always well attended, despite repeated attempts by the Gestapo to close them down. During the summer of 1937 they decided to arrest everyone who turned up. But to their annoyance and frustration, they found that the more people they arrested, the more came to the next service. So in the end they gave up and allowed the gatherings to continue unhindered. As more Christian leaders were arrested, so their names were added to the list of those being prayed for, and the meetings became a vital focus of prayer for the growing number of martyrs of the Confessing Church.

Bible references: Psalm 37:7; Luke 18:1-7; Romans 12:12; Ephesians 6:18-20; Colossians 4:2-3; 1 Thessalonians 5:17; Revelation 6:9-11.

Source: Adapted from Edwin Robertson *The Shame and the Sacrifice* (Hodder and Stoughton, 1987), pp 141-2.

50. Simplicity

(Faith, Hearing God, Loneliness, Old age, Presence of God, Sickness, Silence, Voice of God)

Every day, without fail, the vicar used to see an elderly man come into the church at midday. He'd sit there in silence for five minutes, then get up and go out. After this had been going on for some considerable time, the vicar could contain his curiosity no longer, and he asked the man what it was that brought him in so regularly. The man replied, 'I come in, and I sit down, and I say, "Jesus, it's Jim," and that's all I need to say, 'cos he knows the rest, and he knows what I mean.' Several weeks later the vicar noticed that Jim was missing, and after making a few enquiries he discovered that he had had an accident and had been taken into hospital.

Jim was in a grim and cheerless ward, but he himself was so friendly and cheerful that several of the nurses commented on the way that he'd brightened the place up. One of them actually asked him how he managed to stay so positive. 'It's on account of my visitor, nurse,' he told her. 'But Jim,' she replied, worried that his mind was wandering, 'I've never seen you have any visitors.' 'Oh, yes, nurse,' answered the old man. 'Every day at 12 o'clock, he comes into the ward and he stands by my bed, and he says "Jim, it's Jesus."'

Bible references: 1 Kings 19:11-12; Psalm 23:4; 46:10; 62:1; 121; 123:1-2; Matthew 6:7-8.

Source: Adapted from Roy Etherton, Sevenoaks.

THE CHURCH

51. Anglicans

(Brethren, Cathedrals, Chanting, Liturgy, Service books, Worship, Humour)

'I never went to an Episcopal church before in my life, but there I was in Denmark, and when it comes to worship, the English language has always been real important to me. We didn't speak in tongues in the Plymouth Brethren back in Minnesota, just English, same as our Lord and His Apostles, so I went that Sunday and then every Sunday thereafter....

'Most of the worshippers were Brits, including a bunch of tweed-clad couples in their early seventies who strode in like they'd just killed a fox that morning and knelt down, addressed the Lord, got the thing done and taken care of, and got up and went home to dine on beef.... They were stodgy and warbly and wonderful in every way, and I walked home from Mass feeling rejuvenated, whistling a Fats Waller tune, and making up words to it...:

I'm slow to anger, don't covet or lust.
No sins of pride except sometimes I really must.

Episcopalian, saving my love for you.
The theology's easy, the liturgy too.
Just stand up and kneel down and say what the others do.
Episcopalian, saving my love for you....

'A boy who grew up in the Brethren is an easy mark for the Episcopalians: they march into the dim cathedral chanting ancient things in their beady gowns and blowing smoke at him and next thing you know he is reading prayers out of a book.

I bless myself with a flick of the wrist.
You'd never know I was raised fundamentalist.
Episcopalian, saving my love for you....

'I don't have the manual dexterity to be a true Episcopalian, who must juggle the prayer book, hymnal and the order of service, and sometimes a special mimeographed Kyrie or Sanctus; the music sounds thin and sharp to someone brought up on the Wesleys; the bowing and kneeling are odd – in the Brethren we just clomped in and sat down, and there was no incense in the air, just cologne, and no statuary (though some of our members were less lively than others); and then, if on top of that, the sermon is about revolutionizing our awareness of homeless gay handicapped Nicaraguans, the Episcopal church is more exotic to me than anything in Scandinavia.

There's white folks and black, and gay and morose,
Some male Anglo Saxons but we watch them pretty close.
Episcopalian, saving my love for you.'

Source: Garrison Keillor, *We are Still Married* (Faber and Faber, 1989), pp 204-6.

52. Baptism

(Alcohol, Clergy, Misunderstanding, Humour)

A Highland minister was out visiting one of his parishioners prior to a baptism the following Sunday. When he came to the remote farmhouse he asked the father, 'Are you all prepared for the baptism?' 'Aye,' replied the shepherd, 'I've got a grand ham for the dinner.' 'No, no,' said the minister, 'I mean, are you spiritually prepared?' 'Aye, that, too,' answered the man, 'I've got a quart jar from the inn.'

Source: *Christian Basics Course* (CPAS).

53. Body of Christ

(Commitment, Criticism, Gossip, Service, Humour)

William Wilkerson once said:
    The church is full of bones:
    wish bones – who wish someone else would do the work;
    jaw bones – who talk a lot but do little else;
    knuckle bones – who knock what everyone else does;
    back bones – who get on and actually do the work.

Bible references: Ezekiel 37:1-14; Romans 12:3-8; 1 Corinthians 12; Ephesians 4:11-12, 15-16; Colossians 2:19.

Source: Quoted by John Finney, *The Well Church Book* (Scripture Union, 1991), p 76.

54. Church-going

(Alcohol, Christianity, Drugs, Health, Lifestyle, Science, Sickness, Smoking)

Church services are good for the health, according to a whole series of scientific surveys carried out in the United States. For instance, a survey of 4,000 people in North Carolina found that older people who attended church were less depressed and physically healthier than their less religious counterparts. The study was described to the American Association for the Advancement of Science by Dr Harald Koenig, who said, 'Church-related activity may prevent illness both by a direct effect, using prayer or scripture reading as coping behaviours, as well as by an indirect effect through its influence on health behaviours. For example, active religious participation may indirectly prevent health problems due to poor diet, substance abuse, smoking, self-destructive behaviours, or unsafe sexual practices.'

Dr Dale Matthews of Georgetown University reported that in a review of 212 comparable studies he had found similar results in fully three-quarters, notably those examining substance abuse, alcoholism, mental illness, quality of life, illness, and survival rates. Dr Matthews emphasised that this did not mean that 'prayer should supplant Prozac, or that saints are always healthier than sinners, even though as a group those with religious commitment are healthier.'

Bible references: Hebrews 10:25.

Source: Adapted from the *Daily Telegraph*, 12 March 1996.

55. Church-going

(Alcohol,   Crime,   Drink-driving,   Punishment,   Sabbath, Humour)

In 1993, a Brazilian judge handed down an unusual sentence to a young drink-driver: he was required to attend Mass every Sunday for a year. Paulo dos Santos caused the death of his best friend when he gave him a lift on his motorcycle after a drinking spree. Judge Monoel da Luz instructed the local priest in Varzea Nova, in Paraiba state, to make sure that the young man faithfully attended church, and to report him to the authorities if he failed to turn up.

Bible references: Hebrews 10:25.

Source: Adapted from the *Daily Telegraph*, 24 July 1993.

56. Ecumenism

(Alcohol,   Anglicans,   Baptists,   Confession,   Fellowship, Gossip, Methodists, Sharing, Smoking, Humour)

After an ecumenical Lent course, three of the men from the group decided to go on meeting. One was a Baptist, one a Methodist and the third an Anglican. They found they got on really well together, and shared and prayed together about their faith, their work and their families.

After a few weeks the Methodist said, 'Guys, I really feel I can trust you. We've become such good friends! So I'd like to share with you a particular problem I have. As you probably know, my church really doesn't approve of alcohol. But I can't see anything wrong with the occasional glass of wine, and so I've built up my own little wine cellar in the basement. The thing is, I can't tell anyone at church, so I'd really appreciate your prayers.'

'Isn't that great!' exclaimed the Baptist. 'It's so good that you feel you can share that with us. And it makes me think I can share something very similar. In my church it's smoking that's frowned upon. But I've never seen the harm in the odd cigar now and then. Of course, I can't smoke in the house or I'd get found out, so I keep a little stock in the shed. I do feel bad about it, so it's really helpful to be able to tell you about it.'

'This is wonderful!' said the Anglican. 'Well, I may as well share my problem too. You see, I'm a terrible gossip. I just can't keep a secret. I can't wait to get out of here!'

Bible references: Galatians 6:1-2; James 5:16.

Source: David Macinnes, Cambridge, 1980.

57. History

(Crusades, Middle Ages, Misunderstanding, Reformation, Humour)

A history of the church in the Middle Ages and the Reformation, compiled from papers submitted by freshmen at McMaster University and the University of Alberta in Canada. (The original spelling has been retained!)

During the Middle Ages, everybody was middle aged. Church and state were co-operatic. Middle Evil society was made up of monks, lords and surfs. Mideval people were violent. Murder during this period was nothing. Everybody killed someone. The Crusades were a series of military expaditions made by Christians seeking to free the holy land (the 'Home Town' of Christ) from the Islams. In the 1400 hundreds most Englishmen were perpendicular. Europe was full of incredible churches with great art bulging out their doors. The Middle Ages slimpared to a halt. The renasence bolted in from the blue. Life reeked with joy.

The Reformation happened when German nobles resented the idea that tithes were going to Papal France or the Pope thus enriching Catholic coiffures. Traditions had become oppressive so they too were crushed in the wake of man's quest for ressurection above the not-just-social beast he had become. An angry Martin Luther nailed 95 theocrats to a church door. Theologically, Luthar was into reorientation mutation. Calvinism was the most convenient religion since the days of the ancients. Anabaptist services tended to be migratory. The Popes, of course, were usually Catholic. Monks went right on seeing themselves as worms. The last Jesuit priest died out in the 19th century.

Source: Anders Henriksson, 'A History of the Past: "Life Reeked with Joy"', *WQ*, Winter 1986, pp 149-50.

58. Liturgy

(Bishops, Confirmation, Holy Spirit, Liturgical reform, Presence of God, Responses, Service books, Humour)

The 1970s were a time of great liturgical change in the

Church of England, with different forms of service coming out on a trial basis at regular intervals. Some welcomed the new forms, others had strong reservations. The then Bishop of Kensington is said to have turned up to lead a confirmation service which he began with the words: 'The Lord is here.' In line with the latest liturgy, he was expecting the response: 'His Spirit is with us,' but instead there was a stony silence. He tried again, a little louder: 'The Lord is here!', but again there was no reply from the congregation. So he said it a third time, this time with still greater emphasis. When this once again failed to produce any response from the congregation, he turned to the vicar and said: 'The Lord is here, isn't he?' To which the vicar replied: 'Not in our book he isn't.'

Source: Adapted from Mark Stibbe, London 1996.

59. Numbers

(Church-going, Judaism, Money, Synagogue, Humour)

It is not only various Christian denominations which have been seeing declining numbers at their services, but Jewish synagogues too. In Perth Amboy in New Jersey, the Shaarey Tefiloh Synagogue took decisive steps to buck the trend and boost attendance. They offered $2,500 'welcome presents' to all new recruits, with the additional promise of free school transport and, if necessary, help in finding employment. On request, the synagogue leaders would also arrange a meeting with a local bank manger to discuss attractive loan rates.

Source: Adapted from the *Daily Telegraph*, 17 February 1996.

60. An outsider's perspective

(Baptism, Chanting, Church-going, Confession, Conversion, Faith, Religion, Unbelief)

'I keep thinking, as I settle down into the pew and open and close the hymn book, of a guy I met at the races who told me: "I have let the Lord Jesus into my heart. It just suddenly happened when I went into a church...." So I'm sitting, nervous, also thinking of what somebody else told me, that being worried about God is the thing that happens to you *just* before you get God. So I look at the stained glass windows ... feeling like I'm visiting someone in hospital and trying not to breathe too deeply, trying not to get their germs, and I think: Please let me not get God.

'Will anybody spot me? It's like when you're in a strip club: you think, with relief, well, if they do spot me, *they're* in here too. Organised religion has sunk pretty low these days, at least among people I know; the feeling is that it's just third-raters who get involved, oily little tinpot careerists or neurotics, people afraid of the modern world....

'This is my local church, these mild-looking people must be my neighbours, but I've never seen any of them before; religious people and pagans live in completely different worlds these days. The churchgoers all look like the nicer characters in Australian soaps: calm faces, a permanent half-smile, slightly out-of-date inexpensive clothes....

'And now we're standing up, and ... *chanting*. In unison, like some kind of Masonic rite. I was forced to go to church several times a week at school, but I'd forgotten all this. "So many things we ought not to have done, we have done." The voices have that assured, scary twang to them.

'A ritual is being organised, quite a frightening one, with people standing in formation around the altar, and, my God! Someone's carrying a *baby* towards them! My tabloid-conditioned satanic abuse needle gives a jolt. The woman says …

'"Do you turn to Christ?"

'They chant: "I turn to Christ."

'"Do you renounce evil?"

'"I renounce evil."

'I can't believe this: I'm cringing, I want to escape. What have I got mixed up in here? These people, like druids around a campfire, warding off evil spirits....

'At the end, I'm bolting for the door, pushing a bit, unable to help myself.... Outside the church, the noisy, irreligious world looks great. And no, I didn't get God.'

Bible references: Acts 2:13; 1 Corinthians 14:23.

Source: William Leith, 'I knelt down and prayed that God wouldn't get me', *Independent on Sunday* 1994.

61. Sacraments

(Baptism, Clergy, History, Holy Communion, Humour)

Sometimes we idealise the way things used to be, imagining nineteenth-century churches full of Christians worshipping with commitment and fervour. That this was by no means always the case is evident from the following description of the state of affairs at Fordington when the new vicar arrived in the 1820s, recorded by Francis Kilvert in his *Diaries*.

No man had ever been known to receive the Holy Communion except the parson, the clerk and the sexton.

There were sixteen women communicants and most of them went away when he refused to pay them for coming. They had been accustomed there at some place in the neighbourhood to pass the cup to each other with a nod of the head. At one church there were two male communicants. When the cup was given to the first he touched his forelock and said, 'Here's your good health, sir.' The other said, 'Here's the good health of our Lord Jesus Christ.'

One day there was christening and no water in the font. 'Water, sir!' said the clerk in astonishment. 'The last parson never used no water. He spit into his hand.'

Source: Quoted in A. N. Wilson (ed.) *The Faber Book of Church and Clergy* (Faber and Faber, 1992), pp 156-7.

62. Strange sects

(Bible, End times, Eschatology, Second Coming)

In the United States (where else?) there is apparently a group known as the 'yellers' sect'. They interpret 1 Thessalonians 4:16 ('For the Lord himself shall descend from heaven with a shout') to mean that Christ will only return if they shout loudly enough. As a result, they spend their time yelling out the Lord's name!

Bible references: John 5:25; 1 Thessalonians 4:16.

Source: Adapted from Russell Chandler, *Doomsday* (Word, 1993), pp 24-5.

63. Worship

(Church-going,   Clergy,   History,   Prayer,   Preaching, Responses, Sermon, Young people, Humour)

As L. P. Hartley famously observed, 'The past is a foreign country; they do things differently there.' Just how different church services were is demonstrated by this account by the eighteenth-century cleric and hymn-writer William Cowper:

> If I was concerned to see several distressed pastors, as well as many of our country churches, in a tottering condition, I was more offended with the indecency of worship in others. I could wish that the clergy would inform their congregations, that there is no occasion to scream themselves hoarse in making the responses; that the town-crier is not the only person qualified to pray with due devotion; and that he who bawls the loudest may nevertheless be the wickedest fellow in the parish. The old women too in the aisle might be told, that their time would be better employed in attending to the sermon, than in fumbling over their tattered testaments till they have found the text; by which time the discourse is near drawing to a conclusion: while a word or two of instruction might not be thrown away upon the younger part of the congregation, to teach them that making posies in summer time, and cracking nuts in autumn is no part of the religious ceremony.

Bible references: Isaiah 1:13-14; Amos 4:4-5; 5:21-3.

Source: *Letters and Prose Writings*, quoted in Leslie J. Francis (ed.), *The Country Parson* (Gracewing, 1989), p 107.

CLERGY

64. Disdain

(Church, Food, History, Preaching, Sermons, Status, Work, Humour)

One wonders how widespread was the nineteenth-century perception of the clergy voiced by Miss Crawford, one of Jane Austen's characters:

> What is to be done in the church? Men love to distinguish themselves, and in either of the other lines, distinction may be gained, but not in the church. A clergyman is nothing.... One does not see much of [his] influence and importance in society, and how can it be acquired when they are so seldom seen themselves? How can two sermons a week, even supposing them to be worth hearing ... govern the conduct and fashion the manners of a large congregation for the rest of the week? One scarcely sees a clergyman out of his pulpit....
>
> No doubt he is very sincere in preferring an income ready made to the trouble of working for one; and has the best intentions of doing nothing all the rest of his days but

eat, drink, and grow fat. It is indolence Mr Bertram, indeed. Indolence and love of ease – a want of all laudable ambition, of taste for good company, or of inclination to take the trouble of being agreeable, which makes men clergymen. A clergyman has nothing to do but to be slovenly and selfish – read the newspaper, watch the weather, and quarrel with his wife. His curate does all the work, and the business of his own life is to dine.

Bible references: 1 Corinthians 9:3-14; 1 Thessalonians 5:12-13; 1 Timothy 3:1-13; 5:17-20; Titus 1:5-9; Hebrews 13:7, 17; 1 Peter 5:1-3.

Source: Jane Austen, *Mansfield Park* (Penguin, 1985), pp 120, 136-7.

65. Eccentrics

(Church-going, Dogs, Pastoral care, Preaching)

The Reverend Frederick Densham was vicar of Warleggan, a small village on the edge of Bodmin Moor, from 1931 to 1953. Pastoral care was evidently not one of his strong points: when his parishioners stopped coming to church, he put up a tall barbed-wire fence around the rectory and acquired fierce Alsatian guard dogs. He himself became a virtual recluse, holding services in the now empty church and preaching to wooden and cardboard cut-outs which he placed in the pews!

Bible references: Ezekiel 34:1-6; John 21:15-17; 1 Peter 5:1-3.

Source: *Church of England Newspaper*, 1995.

66. Eccentrics

(Baptism, Cats, Clerical dress, Drugs, Exorcism, History, Sabbath, Humour)

When it comes to eccentric clergy, the nineteenth-century vicar of Morwenstow, Robert Stephen Hawker, was widely renowned for his bizarre habits. He had an aversion to wearing black, so wore claret-coloured coats, which usually hung open to reveal a fisherman's jersey beneath, bedecked with holy medals. Over this he wore a yellow cloak, and knee-length fishing boots completed his striking outfit. On his head he wore a pink or plum-coloured brimless beaver hat. On one occasion he dressed as a mermaid with seaweed tresses, to make a point to his parishioners, and on another excommunicated one of his numerous cats for catching a mouse on a Sunday.

He would prostrate himself full-length during services, and pinch babies during baptisms to make them yell the devil out. He built himself a little hut up above Morwenstow from the timber of wrecked ships, where he could sit undisturbed, smoking pipes of opium and writing poetry.

Bible references: 2 Kings 1:7-8; Matthew 3:4; 11:8; 23:5; Mark 1:6; Luke 7:25.

Source: Adapted from the *Daily Telegraph*, 1995.

67. Example

(Apartheid, Children, Discipleship, Humility, Inequality, Love, Racism, Tolerance)

In South Africa under apartheid, a young black boy was walking beside his mother when a tall white man who was passing greeted them by raising his hat. The boy was amazed. Fancy a white man raising his hat to a black woman! 'Why did he do that?' he asked his mother. 'Because he is a priest,' she replied. 'I want to be a priest,' the boy said. The tall white man was Trevor Huddlestone, then a parish priest in the black Johannesburg suburb of Sophiatown and a tireless opponent of apartheid. The name of the young black boy was Desmond Tutu.

Bible references: Romans 12:10; 1 Corinthians 4:15-16; 11:1; Philippians 2:3-4; 3:17; Colossians 3:12; Titus 3:2; James 3:13; 1 Peter 5:5.

Source: Adapted from Brother Bernard, 1992.

68. Expectations

(Children, Church, Clergy wives, Clerical dress, God, Pram services, Robes, Humour)

The pram service had been lively and well attended. The vicar stood at the door greeting each one in turn as the mothers and children filed out in an orderly, but friendly, fashion. Without warning, he was grabbed from behind by the skirt of his cassock; a small boy cried out triumphantly – 'Gotcha God!'

Before the vicar had caught his breath, the boy turned to the vicar's wife and asked, 'Wot's it like, living with God at the vicarage?'

Bible references: Matthew 23:7-12; Acts 14:11-15.

Source: Wanda Nash, *Living with God at the Vicarage* (Grove Books, 1990), p 2.

69. Expectations

(Discipleship, Example, Goodness, Holiness, Laity, Lifestyle, Sin, Humour)

Samuel Butler's tongue-in-cheek description of the expectations placed on the nineteenth-century clergyman will still ring true to many a modern minister:

> The clergyman is expected to be a kind of human Sunday. Things must not be done in him which are venial in the week-day classes. He is paid for this business of leading a stricter life than other people. It is his *raison d'être*. If his parishioners feel that he does this they approve of him, for they look upon him as their own contribution towards what they deem a holy life. This is why the clergyman is so often called a 'vicar' – he being the person whose vicarious goodness is to stand for that of those entrusted to his charge.

Bible references: Matthew 7:1-5; Luke 6:41-2; 1 Corinthians 4:1-4; James 3:1.

Source: Samuel Butler, *The Way of All Flesh* (Everyman, 1965), pp 98-9.

70. Gambling

(Bequests, Bible, Eccentrics, Guidance, Luck, Prayer)

Paul Sebastian was an eccentric minister at St Ives in Cornwall in the nineteenth century. He bequeathed a sum of money to his chapel in his will of 1829 with the following provision:

> That the money provide six Bibles every year, for which six men and six women are to throw dice on Whit Tuesday after the morning service, the minister kneeling the while at the south end of the communion table, and praying to God to direct the luck to his glory.

Bible references: Leviticus 16:8-10; Numbers 26:55-6; 1 Samuel 14:41-2; Acts 1:24-6.

Source: Quoted in *Tombstone Humour* (Chancellor Press, 1993), p 160.

71. Hymns

(Choirs, Music, Organists, Singing, Worship, Humour)

The vicar was one of those who like to show how broadminded they are by working regardlessly through almost every hymn in the book – and some outside as well. And the choir was one of those who only know about a dozen tunes which have been handed down from generation to generation, and strongly object to learning anything else. Consequently a most keen and enjoyable contest had developed between the vicar and the organist. The vicar would dig up an unknown hymn, and the organist would endeavour to fit it to one of the choir's accepted tunes. The organist and choir had never been beaten, but once they had been in grave danger of losing a point. The vicar had discovered a hymn written in such an extraordinary metre that it refused to be married off to an eligible tune.

Things looked black, and it became obvious that the choir would have to do the unthinkable and learn a new tune. However, at the last moment the vicar was taken ill with 'flu, and a relieving priest had been prevailed upon to substitute 'Onward Christian Soldiers'.

Source: Reginal Frary, *Don't Upset the Choir*, quoted in Leslie J. Francis (ed.) *The Country Parson* (Gracewing, 1989), pp 108-9.

72. Robes

(Clerical dress, Misunderstanding, Humour)

A clergyman from Winchester was staying at a London hotel for the night, as he was due to be taking part in a service in the capital the following day. He had reserved the room rather late, and had been obliged to book a double room. He couldn't be bothered to unpack his suitcase before dinner, but left it with his robe case in the room. When he came back, he was rather surprised to find his pyjamas neatly laid out on one side of the bed, and his surplice spread out on the other!

Source: Adapted from Michael Green, *The Peterborough Book* (Sphere, 1982), pp 49-50.

73. Sex

(Conferences, Holidays, Misunderstanding, School, Humour)

A group of clergy touring Australia were accommodated in one town in the dormitories of a girls' school, which was empty because it was the school holidays. They were amused to find a notice by the bed: 'If you require a mistress during the night, please ring the bell'.

Source: Michael Green, *The Peterborough Book* (Sphere, 1982), p 29.

74. Status

(Archbishop, History, Humility, Persecution, Reformation, Servanthood)

In 1556 Thomas Cranmer, formerly Archbishop of Canterbury but now removed from office by Mary Tudor on account of his Protestant theology, was solemnly defrocked. The eminent Reformation historian Gordon Rupp comments:

> And when at last he stood unfrocked, dressed in the clothes of a poor bargeman, Bonner [Bishop of London] cried out, 'Now you are Lord no more.'... And when all the layers had been removed, an Archbishop had at last been revealed 'in the form of a servant' – i.e. the only holy garments ever assumed by the Lord and Maker of the Church.

Bible references: Matthew 20:25-7; 23:11-12; Mark 9:35; 10:42-4; John 13:3-5; Philippians 2:5-8; Colossians 3:12; 1 Peter 5:5.

Source: Quoted in F. F. Bruce, *The Gospel of John* (Eerdmans, 1983), p 280.

75. Uncertainty

(Belief, Christianity, Evangelism, Faith, Incarnation, Liberalism, Modernity, Resurrection, Virgin birth)

'When researching my play about inner London priesthood [*Racing Demon*], I was astonished to meet a supremely dedicated group of men who barely mentioned, let alone spread the gospel.... They served honourably as society's trouble-shooters, doing what was to all intents and purposes social work, and all on a half of even a social worker's pay. But at no time did it seem part of their agenda to mention to the people they were helping that every Sunday, in another costume perhaps, they conducted services which related, however loosely, to a much-discussed incident in the Middle East 2,000 years ago.

'The experience of meeting these good souls left me confused, because although I liked them ... it did seem to me, as an outsider, that they were perhaps overlooking some essential point about the Christian religion. If Christ did rise from the dead, then call me a fanatic, but I think you probably do have to tell people about it. The inner city priest's conviction that the poor, for some reason, don't need to be brought up to speed on the news, does seem to be vaguely insulting. The Christian faith, after all, is based on the idea of intervention. Mankind is bowling along, following its own sinful ways, and then once and for all the physical rules of the universe are suspended and God intervenes. I cannot see how if the facts of Christ's life are true, they do not change everything....

'Although you may want to believe that Christianity's message may be boiled down to something – however vague – to do with love and its operations in the world, its authority does have to depend on two central claims, which no amount of modernist wriggling can quite dispose of. Christians are people who believe, first, that a man was born of a virgin. And if you ask for a doctor's chitty to excuse you believing even that one, nobody is going to let you off what I think we may insist is the Christian dealbreaker: that a corpse did walk out of a tomb.

'These two claims seem to me historically to have exerted such a powerful hold over the human imagination that you cannot simply dump them for jetsam at the end of the twentieth century. It is not just that they are part of the ship. Without them, I'm not sure you have any ship at all.'

Bible references: Matthew 1:18-25; 28:1-10, 17; Mark 16:1-8; Luke 1:30-5; 24:1-43; John 1:13; 20:1-31; Acts 2:24, 32; 13:30-7; 17:31-2; Romans 1:3-4; 1 Corinthians 15:1-8, 12-20; 1 Peter 1:21.

Source: Adapted from David Hare, 'Why I don't believe', the *Daily Telegraph*, 13 July 1996.

76. Unlikely Messiahs – H. J. Prince

(Anglicans, Christ, Church, Eccentrics, History, Holy Spirit, Immortality, Jesus, Sects, Sex)

In 1841, H. J. Prince, curate of Charlinch in Somerset, sparked off a revival in the parish church. He was a charismatic personality and a gifted orator, and his rector, the

Rev. Starkey, soon became a devoted follower. When Prince preached at Sunday services he whipped the normally stolid congregation of farmers, labourers and their families into a frenzy; men quaked, women screamed and even small children were affected.

All this soon came to the attention of the Bishop of Bath and Wells, who repeatedly tried to stop what was happening. Disillusioned with the Church of England, Starkey and Prince left to set up an independent religious community in the nearby village of Spaxton, the Agapemone, or Abode of Love, where Prince built a grand country house. He was not lacking in wealthy backers, particularly women such as the four Nottidge sisters, three of whom Prince married to male disciples, the fourth being committed to an asylum by her family to keep her out of Prince's clutches. She nonetheless managed to escape to join the others.

In time, Prince announced that he was united with the Holy Ghost and therefore immortal. God had also revealed to him that Jesus was just one in a long line of redeemers, beginning with Adam and Noah and culminating, not surprisingly, in Prince himself. Having been blessed with immortality, Prince revealed that his task was to pass that blessing on to his disciples.

The first to be so blessed was Sister Zoe Paterson, with whom he publicly consummated his divine union on a sofa in the billiard room, in front of the other brothers and sisters. Prince also told his followers that now that sexual intercourse had become a holy sacrament, God would render his servants sterile. It therefore came as a shock to everyone when Sister Zoe became pregnant. Prince tried to get around this difficulty by reporting that God had told him that this was a child of Satan, sent to undermine his work, but support soon began to wane, and financial contributions from outside fell off sharply.

Prince lived on till 1899, when he was succeeded as self-styled Messiah by the Rev. T. H. Smyth Pigott, who announced his own divinity in 1902, and went on to sire two children called Power and Glory.

Bible references: Matthew 7:15-20; 24:5, 23-4; Mark 13:21-2; Luke 17:23; 21:8; 2 Peter 2:1-3; 1 John 4:1.

Source: Adapted from Peter Washington, *Madame Blavatsky's Baboon* (Secker and Warburg, 1993), pp 5-7.

SERMONS AND PREACHING

77. Adaptability

(Baptism, Clergy, Confirmation, Harvest, Humour)

'My sermon on the meaning of the manna in the wilderness can be adapted to almost any occasion, joyful, or, as in the present case, distressing. I have preached it at harvest celebrations, christenings, confirmations, on days of humiliation and festal days. The last time I delivered it was in the Cathedral, as a charity sermon on behalf of the Society for the Prevention of Discontent Among the Upper Orders. The Bishop, who was present, was much struck by some of the analogies I drew.'

Bible references: Exodus 16:11-36; Numbers 11:4-9; Revelation 2:17.

Source: Dr Chasuble in Oscar Wilde, *The Importance of Being Earnest*, Act 2.

87

78. Boredom

(Children, Church, Misunderstanding, Humour)

A small boy was sitting beside his father during a long, dull sermon. Spotting the red glow of a sanctuary lamp in a side chapel, he whispered to his father, 'Dad, when the light goes green, can we go?'

Source: Michael Green, *The Peterborough Book* (Sphere, 1982), p 38.

79. Boredom

(Church, Listening, Humour)

In his book, *Evangelism for a New Age*, John Drane quotes a piece of research which reveals that no fewer than 42 per cent of British churchgoers admitted to having fallen asleep during a service. More than a third said that they looked at their watch in church every Sunday, while fully 10 per cent owned up to having put their watch to their ear and shaken it in the belief that it must have stopped.

Bible references: Acts 20:7-12.

Source: Review in the *Church of England Newspaper*, 1994.

80. Commandments

(Bible, Clergy, Dishonesty, Laity, Stealing, Unpopularity)

In the Old West, the minister of a frontier town was out for a walk by the river one day when he saw a number of members of his congregation down by the water's edge, dragging some logs ashore. He could see that each log had the owner's name stamped on the end, and he was horrified to see his church members bringing out their saws and cutting off the end with the tell-tale mark. He resolved that he could not let the matter pass.

So the following Sunday he preached a powerful sermon on the commandment, 'Thou shalt not steal.' But to his dismay, one after another of the people he'd seen down by the river shook him by the hand as they left the church, saying things like, 'Mighty fine sermon, pastor,' or, 'That was a wonderful message.' The pastor spent the week pondering his next move, and in the end decided on his plan of action. The following Sunday he preached exactly the same sermon as the previous week, word for word, until the very end. As he summed up, instead of saying, 'And so, my friends, the Bible is clear: Thou shalt not steal,' as he had the previous week, he said: 'And so, my friends, the Bible is clear: Thou shalt not cut the end off thy neighbour's logs.' They ran him out of town.

Bible references: Exodus 20:15; Leviticus 19:11; Deuteronomy 5:19; Matthew 7:21-3; 19:17-27; Mark 10:19; Luke 6:46-9; 18:20; Romans 13:9; James 1:22-5.

Source: Adapted from Haddon Robinson, in *Mastering Contemporary Preaching* (Multnomah Press, 1989), pp 63-4.

81. Conversion

(Church,   Clergy,   Conviction,   Criticism,   Evangelists, Repentance, Humour)

'Bernie Tollefson came to church one Sunday night on a dare from his chums and sat in back and *smirked* at Rev. Osterhus until the evangelist would stand it no longer – he leaped from the pulpit! Dashed to the back pew! Seized the young man by the neck before he could slither away! Hauled him out and up to the altar! Threw him against the rail! The sinner fell weeping to the floor, and the man of God knelt over him, one knee in the small of his back, and prayed ferociously for light to dawn in his blackened soul. When Bernie stood up, he was reborn, and he yelled, "Thank you, Jesus!" over and over, tears pouring down his cheeks – "Now *there* was what I call preaching!" says ... Bernie's brother, a deacon and Pastor Ingqvist's faithful critic.

'He says of the pastor's sermons, "He mumbles. He murmurs. It's a lot of on-the-one-hand-this, on-the-other-hand-that. He never comes straight out. He never puts the hay down where the goats can get it. It's a lot of talk, and many a Sunday I've walked away with no idea *what* he said. Can't remember even where he started from. You never had that problem with the old preachers. There was never a moment's doubt. It was Repent or Be Damned. We need that. This guy, he tries to please everybody. Just once I wish he'd raise his voice and pound on the pulpit. That way I'd know he wasn't talking in his sleep."'

Bible references: Acts 9:28-9; 14:3; Galatians 1:10; 1 Thessalonians 2:4.

Source: Garrison Keillor, *Lake Wobegon Days* (Faber and Faber, 1986), p 320.

82. Criticism

(Boredom, Church, Clergy, History)

'There is perhaps, no greater hardship at present inflicted on mankind in civilised and free countries, than the necessity of listening to sermons. No one but a preaching clergyman has in these realms the power of compelling an audience to sit silent and be tormented. No one but a preaching clergyman can revel in platitudes, truisms and untruisms and yet receive as his undisputed privilege, the same respectful demeanour as though words of impassioned eloquence, or persuasive logic, fell from his lips…. He is the bore of the age … the nightmare that disturbs our Sunday rest, the incubus that loads our religion and makes God's service distasteful!'

Source: Anthony Trollope, quoted in James A. Feehan, *Preaching in Stories* (Mercier Press, 1989), pp 11-12.

83. Humility

(Clergy, Laity, Word of God, Humour)

A woman came up to the preacher at the end of the service and shook his hand warmly. 'Thank you, pastor,' she said. 'That was a truly wonderful message, absolutely excellent.' With true Christian humility the pastor replied modestly, 'Well it wasn't me speaking, of course, it was the Lord.' 'Oh no,' she responded immediately. 'It wasn't *that* good.'

Bible references: Acts 2:4; 13:46; 1 Corinthians 2:12-13; 2 Corinthians 13:3; Philippians 1:14.

Source: Quoted by Stuart Briscoe, in *Mastering Contemporary Preaching* (Multnomah Press, 1989), p 142.

84. Judgement

(Church-going, Hell, History, Humour)

Bishop Hilary of Arles once shouted at those who were leaving church before the sermon, 'You won't get out of hell so easily!' Caesarius, his sixth-century successor, was more direct: he had the church doors locked once everyone was inside.

Source: Adapted from Edward James, *The Origins of France* (Macmillan, 1982), p 54.

85. Listening

(Boredom, Hymns, Numbers, Worship, Humour)

The Venerable Wallis Thomas, looking back over his long preaching ministry, recalled one man in Bangor Cathedral who, as soon as the sermon began, fixed his eyes on the hymn numbers, where they remained until the sermon ended. When he eventually asked the man why he did this, the man replied that he added all the numbers together and then worked out the square root of the total.

Source: Adapted from the *Daily Telegraph*, 29 August 1994.

86. Listening

(Boredom, Parables, Humour)

'Clarence checked out of Pastor Ingqvist's sermon early. It was about the parable of the labourers in the vineyard, the ones who came late getting the same wage as those who came early and stayed all day, a parable that suggests you need not listen carefully to the whole sermon from the beginning but can come in for maybe the last sentence or two and get the whole point.'

Bible references: Matthew 20:1-16.

Source: Garrison Keillor, *Leaving Home* (Faber and Faber, 1987), p 82.

87. Preaching manuals

(Pulpit exchange, Remembrance, Sermon outlines, Visiting preacher)

A minister in Southampton used to buy an American preaching manual each year, which gave sermon outlines for the year ahead. He found it extremely helpful, and the congregation clearly appreciated the finished product.

To his great delight, he was offered the opportunity to do a ministerial exchange with a pastor in the United States, whereby he would take over the American minister's church for a period, and the colleague take charge of his own church. It all went very well, and because this was a different congregation, he was even able to reuse many of his old sermons, suitably adapted for the new cultural context.

When it came to Veterans' Day, he looked out his sermon from the previous Remembrance Sunday, which he recalled had been particularly well received. To his growing confusion, many people remarked on their way out, 'It's quite remarkable, pastor, but our own minister preached almost exactly the same message last year.' It was only when he got home that he discovered his mistake: his host had written the sermon outline in his preaching manual.

Source: Charles Coupland.

88. Unpopularity

(Church and state, Citizenship, Clergy, Courage, History, War)

Many preachers know how nerve-racking it can be to deliver an unpopular message, but Anglican clergyman Jonathan Boucher found himself in a particularly uncomfortable position in the North American colonies in July 1775. Tensions were running high, and the pro-Independence Continental Congress had called for a day of prayer and fasting to decide on whether – and how – to challenge British authority. Most preachers used the opportunity to speak up for the colonial cause, but Boucher told his congregation that they should submit to the constituted authorities. Aware of how unpopular such a message would be, he carried a loaded pistol into the pulpit with him.

Bible references: 1 Kings 18:16-17; Jeremiah 26:8-15; 38:1-6; Amos 7:12-15; Matthew 10:28; Luke 12:4-5; Romans 13:1-

5; 1 Corinthians 2:3; Galatians 1:10; 1 Thessalonians 2:4.

Source: Adapted from *Christian History*, issue 50.

89. Visiting preacher

(Boredom, Clergy, Listening, Humour)

A visiting preacher had just begun his sermon when he noticed a button in the pulpit. Consumed with curiosity, a couple of minutes later he dared to press it, intrigued to see what would happen. To his amazement the effect on the congregation was almost instantaneous: people sat up, smiled, and looked as if they were really enjoying his preaching. He happily continued with his sermon, but soon noticed that the effect of pressing the button was rapidly wearing off. Some people's eyes had glazed over, others were fidgeting and restless. So he pressed the button again, and once again, to his astonishment and delight, the same thing happened. The congregation was suddenly alert and attentive again, listening to what he had to say. But just a few minutes later he could sense that he was losing them again. Restlessness was spreading, some people were muttering, others even tapping their watches impatiently. He tried the button again, but this time, to his dismay, with little if any effect. He pressed it once, twice more, but still no effect – if anything, the murmuring in the pews actually increased. By now thoroughly rattled, he rushed through the rest of his sermon, missed out his final point, and swiftly brought the sermon to a conclusion.

After the service, at the door, he asked a churchwarden what the button in the pulpit was for. 'Didn't you notice on your way in?' asked the warden, pointing at the pulpit. And there, over the preacher's head, was an illuminated sign reading: 'One more minute'.

Source: Simon Coupland.

FAITH, HOPE AND LOVE

90. Faith

(God, Holocaust, Hope, Jews, Love, Persecution, Silence of God, Suffering)

The following poem was found in a cave in Cologne where a number of Jews had taken refuge from the Nazis:

I believe in the sun
though it is late in rising;
I believe in love
though it is absent;
I believe in God
though he is silent.

Bible references: Job; Psalm 10:1; 13:1-4; 22:1-11; 35:22; 38:21; 42:1-10; 43:2; 77:7-9; 88:14; Isaiah 8:17; Matthew 27:46; Mark 15:34; 2 Corinthians 4:7-18; Hebrews 11:1.

Source: Review of Hilda Schiff (ed.), *Holocaust Poetry* in the *Daily Telegraph*, 1995.

91. Faith

(Life, Perseverance, Water)

There is in Germany a drinking fountain with the inscription on the bowl, 'Come and drink.' The problem is that when you come closer, it quickly becomes apparent that there is no tap, no lever, no handle to be seen anywhere on it. At that point some people give up and go away frustrated and thirsty. The secret is that you have to lean forward in faith, and at that moment a hidden beam will be broken, and a jet of water will spurt up for you to drink.

Bible references: Isaiah 12:3; 44:3; 55:1; Jeremiah 2:13; John 4:10, 14; 7:37-39; Revelation 22:17.

Source: Adapted from David Watson, Cambridge, 11 February 1979.

92. Faith

(The Cross, Crucifixion, Jesus, Testimony, Unbelief, Uncertainty)

'At the age I am now, Jesus' life was finished. He had either completed an extraordinary mission or had been pointlessly and tragically executed. The end is either Christ's last cry of desolation in Luke: "My God, my God, why have you forsaken me?" or it is the certainty of the words, "Father, into your hands I commend my spirit." I don't know. I've sat in churches thinking this is all rubbish. I've thought the mocker's thoughts. And at other times, I have felt that this is all there is. I don't know. I don't know.'

Bible references: Matthew 27:39-44, 46; Mark 15:29-32, 34; Luke 23:35, 46.

Source: Ian Hislop, editor of *Private Eye*, quoted in Nigel McCulloch, *Barriers to Belief* (Darton, Longman and Todd, 1994), pp 26-7.

93. Faith

(Children, Family, Father, God, Protection, Sons)

Two famous botanists were once touring the glens of Scotland in search of rare specimens to add to their collections, when one of them spotted a quite remarkable flower. The problem was that it was growing down in a deep gully, completely inaccessible to them. So they searched out the nearest village and found a local lad whom they thought might be willing to be lowered down on a rope and pick the flower for them. They offered him ten shillings, a handsome sum, if he would help them out. 'I'll not do it for ten shillings,' he replied, so they offered him fifteen, then even a pound. When they realised that he wouldn't budge, they asked him what would persuade him to go down into the gulley for them. 'I'll only do it if my father is holding the end of the rope,' he replied. So they went to see the father, explained the situation, and the father willingly agreed to help. The boy then went down on the rope, picked the botanists' flowers, and brought them safely to the surface. He knew his father wouldn't let him fall.

Bible references: Exodus 33:15-16; Deuteronomy 31:6;

Psalm 31:14-15; 62:5-8; 66:8-9; 94:17-19; 115:9-11; 118:6-7; 121; John 10:28-9; Hebrews 13:5-6.

Source: Adapted from Daniel Cozens, Cambridge, 31 January 1982.

94. Simple faith

(Children, Conversion, Death, Evangelism, Salvation, Shepherds, Suffering)

During his travels around the north of Yorkshire, an evangelist came across a rather simple shepherd boy, and wanted to share the gospel with him. But the local people said he was wasting his time: the lad was that simple he was only fit to look after the sheep, and he certainly couldn't understand the preacher's message about sin and salvation. But the evangelist saw things differently, so he spent some time with the boy, and taught him to say 'The Lord is my shepherd,' and as he did so, to count off the words on the fingers of his left hand. He taught the shepherd boy that the Lord really was his shepherd, and so he told him that when he got to the word 'my', the lad was to enfold that finger in the palm of his other hand, to show how safe and secure he was in God's loving care. The boy seemed to understand, but who could tell?

That winter was a harsh one, and up on the hills the snow fell thickly, leaving the remoter parts of the countryside cut off for several days. When at last the weather eased, people realised that the shepherd boy must have been caught out in the snow. The search party eventually found him, huddled in the snow, cold and stiff. But there was one strange thing they couldn't understand. They found his right hand so tightly clasped around the third finger of his left hand that they were unable to prise his hands apart.

Bible references: Psalm 23; Isaiah 40:11; Ezekiel 34:11-16; Micah 5:4; Matthew 9:36; John 10:1-16, 27-9; Hebrews 13:20; 1 Peter 2:25; 5:4; Revelation 7:17.

Source: Adapted from Daniel Cozens, Cambridge 1980.

95. Faith

(Belief, Children, Families, Father, Humour)

After a visit to the dentist, a little girl carefully put the tooth he'd extracted under her pillow before she went to sleep. Her mother was amused. 'Do you still believe in the tooth fairy, then, darling?' she asked. 'Of course not!' replied the daughter, 'but I still believe in Daddy.'

Source: Adapted from Michael Green, *The Peterborough Book* (Sphere, 1982), p 103.

96. Hope

(Experience, Life, Optimism, Pessimism, Humour)

We have all heard about the glass being half-full or half-empty, but here are some variations on the theme:

- An optimist looks at an oyster and expects to find a pearl; a pessimist looks at an oyster and expects food poisoning.
- A pessimist is someone who feels bad when he feels good, for fear he will feel worse when he feels better.
- A priest travelling on a bus found himself next to a hippy wearing only one shoe. 'I see you lost a shoe,' he said. 'No,' replied the hippy, 'I found one.'
- The optimist proclaims that we live in the best of all possible worlds. And the pessimist fears this is true.

Bible references: Romans 5:5; 8:24-5; 15:13; 1 Corinthians 15:9; Ephesians 1:18; Colossians 1:5; 1 Thessalonians 4:13; Hebrews 6:18-19; 1 Peter 1:3.

Source: Barbara Johnson, *Splashes of Joy in the Cesspools of Life* (Word, 1992), pp 16-17; James A. Feehan, *Preaching in Stories* (The Mercier Press, 1989), p 91; Ruth Rendell, *Put on by Cunning* (Arrow Books, 1994), p 156.

97. Hope

(Children, Darkness, Light, Mission)

The young Robert Louis Stevenson was looking out of the window one evening at the Edinburgh street in which he lived, when the old-fashioned lamplighter came past on his rounds. The boy's nurse called him to come and have his supper, but he couldn't bear to tear himself away from this remarkable sight. 'Look, look!' he cried, his face pressed against the glass, 'There's a man out there punching holes in the darkness.'

Bible references: Genesis 1:3; Job 29:3; Psalm 18:28; Isaiah 9:2; Matthew 4:16; 5:14-16; Luke 2:32; John 1:4-5, 9; 3:19-21; 5:35; 8:12; 9:5; 12:35-6; Acts 13:47; 26:17-18; 2 Corinthians 4:6; 2 Peter 1:19; 1 John 2:8.

Source: Quoted in the *Daily Telegraph*, Spring 1996.

98. Love

(Forgiveness, Friendship, Goodness, Intolerance, Politics, Reconciliation, War)

During the American Civil War, President Abraham Lincoln was once taken to task for the generous attitude he adopted towards the Confederate states. After all, he had said in a speech, the Southerners were human beings, too, were they not? An elderly lady in the audience was incensed by Lincoln's tolerance, and asked the President how he could possibly speak kindly of his enemies when he should be doing everything in his power to destroy them.

'What, madam?' Lincoln replied. 'Do I not destroy my enemies when I make them my friends?'

Bible references: Matthew 5:43-8; Luke 6:27-36; Romans 12:14, 17-21; 1 Peter 4:8; 1 John 2:9-11; 4:7-11.

Source: Adapted from Geoffrey Regan, *Histrionics* (Robson Books, 1994), p 177.

99. Love

(Autism, Children, Embrace, Hugs, Mothers, Parents, Relationships)

One of the main problems in trying to help autistic children is the fact that they live in a world of their own, locked in on themselves, refusing contact with others, even eye contact with their mothers. One of the most successful treatments that has been developed is called the 'holding treatment.' Mothers are encouraged to hold their children lovingly but firmly, trying to look them in the eye. The children resist this, writhing and squirming to break free, avoiding eye contact at all cost.

But when at last the child gives in, stops fighting, and returns the mother's gaze, sometimes after literally hours of struggling, the rewards are glorious. A great sense of peace comes over child and mother, and the two of them are now locked in an embrace of love rather than a battle of wills. In many instances this breakthrough marks the beginning of an improvement in the child's condition and a new relationship between themselves and the world around them.

Bible references: Genesis 32:24-31; Hebrews 12:7-13.

Source: Adapted from Mark Hargreaves, Ridley Hall, 1990.

100. Love

(Beggars, Christ, Church, Grace, Humility, Poverty, Prejudice, Salvation, Servanthood, Singing, Worship)

Marilyn Schlitt was at church in the Philippines one Sunday

morning when something unusual happened. The congregation, dressed in their Sunday best, were heartily singing a
worship song, 'Oh Lord, you're beautiful; your face is all I
see,' when an unknown woman walked in. Her hair was
unkempt, her clothes tattered and her feet muddy. And she
smelt. The singing continued, but all eyes were on this beggar
woman as she shuffled towards the front of the church.
Finally she got there, and to the shocked surprise of the
congregation, the worship leader put his arms around her and,
with tears streaming down his face, hugged her. Somehow
people kept singing, 'And when your eyes are on this child,
your grace abounds to me.'

When the astonished onlookers sat down, Basil, who was
leading the service, told them the whole story. He had been
out for a walk one day when he saw this woman carrying a
bag of rubbish. Feeling compassion, he stopped and asked her
name, and she needed no further prompting to tell him her
sorry situation. She and her unemployed husband were
destitute, their children didn't care about them, and life was a
lonely, wretched drudgery. He told her about the love of God,
a God who cares for the destitute, the lonely and the unloved,
and invited her to the service that Sunday.

The explanations over, Basil took her by the arm as if she
was a rich, upper-class lady, and showed her to a chair in the
front row. Marilyn commented, 'I felt I had been slapped in
the face. All I had seen was a rank, smelly intruder who had
barged in and broken the atmosphere of beauty and worship.
Watching Basil, I saw how Christ would have treated this
poor woman with compassion and dignity. Whatever she had
discovered in this small church meeting, I know what I had
discovered. An ugly prejudice was inside of me that I didn't
know was there. I asked for forgiveness and heard these
words in my heart: "And when your eyes are on this child,
your grace abounds to me."'

Bible references: Leviticus 19:15; Matthew 25:31-46; Luke 16:19-31; Acts 10:34; 1 Corinthians 1:26-8; James 2:1-17.

Source: Adapted from *Renewal*, March 1992.

101. Love

(Death, Families, Forgiveness, Murder, Peace, Reconciliation, Violence)

It was in Belfast. A young woman was locking up the church hall after taking her Sunday School class. Life was good: she had just graduated from university and got engaged; her one great sadness was that her father had recently died. A young man walked up to her. 'Karen?' 'Yes,' she answered. 'I've come for you,' he said, and pulled out a gun. 'But there must be some mistake,' she said. 'No mistake,' he answered, and fired.

As Karen lay dying in her hospital bed, her mother weeping by her bedside, Karen said, 'I know you're broken-hearted for me, mum, but just think of the mothers of the boys who do such things. Think how they must feel.' And she gestured to her Bible and said, 'I want you to find one of these terrorists and give him my Bible. And I want you to tell him that I love them.'

A week later there was a meeting in the Wellington Hall in Belfast. The main speaker was an American named Charles Colson. He'd been involved in the Watergate break-in, and had been to prison for it. There he'd become a Christian, and he now went on speaking engagements across the world, telling people about the love of Christ, and preaching a message of hope and reconciliation. The speaker before him was Liam McClusky, a former member of the Provisional IRA. While he had been in the Maze prison he'd been on a dirty protest for over three years, refusing to wear clothes and smearing his cell with excrement. He'd also been one of the IRA hunger strikers, going without food for fifty-five days, in fact the only one to survive. The only reason that he'd lived was because when he was blinded by lack of food and too weak to resist, his mother had force-fed him. But now he had become a Christian and renounced violence, sharing with others what the love of Christ had done for him.

Just as Colson was about to speak, there was a security alert. A lady was walking up the aisle with her hand in a bag. A security guard rushed forward, but it was all right – as she took her hand out of the bag, it was only a book. She went up to the platform and embraced Liam McClusky. 'This week I've lost a daughter,' she said, 'but tonight I've gained a son.' And Karen's mother told her story. Charles Colson took the microphone and said to the assembled gathering, 'Nothing I could say to you would speak more powerfully than what you have just seen.'

Bible references: Song of Songs 8:6-7; Isaiah 9:6; Matthew 5:43-5; Luke 6:27-31; 23:34; John 15:18-20; Acts 7:60; Romans 8:35-9; 12:14; 1 Corinthians 13:4-8; 2 Corinthians 5:17-21; Galatians 3:26-8; Ephesians 2:14-17; Colossians 3:11.

Source: Adapted from David Armstrong, Cambridge 1986.

DISCIPLESHIP

102. Citizenship

(Church and state, Freedom, History, Nazism, Patriotism, Sacrifice, War)

In the summer of 1939, the German pastor and theologian Dietrich Bonhoeffer was in America, but decided he had to return to Germany. He explained his decision in this profoundly insightful letter to Reinhard Niebuhr:

I must live through this difficult period of our national history with the Christian people of Germany. I will have no right to participate in the reconstruction of Christian life in Germany after the war if I do not share the trials of this time with my people.... Christians in Germany will face the terrible alternative of either willing the defeat of their nation in order that Christian civilisation may survive, or willing the victory of their nation and thereby destroying our civilisation. I know which of these alternatives I must choose.

Bible references: Jeremiah 32; Matthew 20:17-19; 26:39-46;

Mark 10:32-4; 14:35-42; Luke 9:51; 18:31-3; 22:41-2; John 12:23-8; Acts 20:22-4; 21:10-14.

Source: Quoted in Edwin Robertson, *The Shame and the Sacrifice* (Hodder and Stoughton, 1987), p 172.

103. Commitment

(Body of Christ, Church, Fellowship, Gifts, Servanthood, Service, Talents)

Bill Hybels, pastor of Willow Creek Community Church in Chicago, has written:

> When you really love the Church, then you've got to be a part of it, and you've got to die to self and live for Christ through the Church. Once people hear enough of that teaching and sense in our hearts that we really feel that way, then you get that feeling of abandonment sweeping over the church, and you have people who say with great joy, 'Whatever it takes.'
>
> It was thirty-one degrees below zero one night last winter, and we had thirty-five lay people out directing traffic in our parking lot before and after a service. They didn't get a dime for doing it. They huddled together and held hands and thanked God for the privilege of serving in his church. That's whatever it takes.

Bible references: Matthew 20:25-8; Mark 9:35; 10:42-5; Romans 6:6; 12:3-12; 1 Corinthians 12; Philippians 2:5-8.

Source: Quoted in Martin Robinson, *A World Apart* (Monarch, 1992), pp 133-4.

104. Forgiveness

(Apartheid, Hatred, Holy Communion, Love, Peace, Politics, Prison, Racism, Reconciliation, Sacraments)

In his book, *The Life God Blesses*, Gordon Macdonald describes his encounter with a black South African, a high-ranking member of the African National Congress. He was profoundly impressed by the man's understanding of African history and politics and his insight into the challenges facing his nation, and so he asked, 'Where did you get your training?' He expected to hear the name of some famous university, and was amazed at the reply: 'I trained on Robben Island.' This was the notorious offshore prison where the apartheid regime sent its most troublesome opponents. 'Every few years the government would search out and jail all the young black leaders. They would sweep them out of sight and eventually dump them on Robben Island. But for us it was a profitable strategy. Because that was where we got our education. From Mandela and the others.... You see, all of us who came to Robben Island came straight from school. We were angry; we were ready to kill the white man, any white man.

'In prison we lost our names; we were only numbers to the guards. And they kept their guns pointed at us all the time. Each morning we marched to the rock quarry, and in the evening we marched back. The days always belonged to the guards. But the nights were different. The nights belonged to us. During the evening, we who were young sat with the old men. And we listened while they told us their histories, their tribal languages, their dreams for the black person in South Africa.

'But most important, Mandela taught us that you can never accomplish anything as long as you hate your enemy. Hate his politics; hate the evil behind those politics; hate the policies that put you in prison. But never hate the person. It takes your strength away.'

'You stopped hating?' Macdonald asked.

'Not right away. It took me almost five years to forgive ... five years of learning with the old men. But when I did forgive, I was a different person. I knew I had forgiven when I could go to Holy Communion on Friday and invite the guard to lay down his gun, come and receive the sacrament with me. So that's the answer to your question. That's where I got my training.'

Bible references: Matthew 5:23-4, 43-8; Luke 6:27-36; 23:34; Acts 7:60; Romans 12:9, 14, 17-21; 1 Corinthians 10:16-17; 2 Corinthians 5:17-21; Galatians 3:26-8; Ephesians 2:14-17; Colossians 3:11; 1 John 2:9-11; 4:19-21.

Source: Adapted from *Renewal*, July 1995.

105. Forgiveness

(Church, Revenge, Singing, Worship, Humour)

'When the praise session arrived, it threatened never to go away again. Those musicians and singers got completely carried away and gave us a real foretaste of eternity. An exaggeration of course – it only lasted about three days. By the time I got up to speak, everyone was exhausted. I forgave the music group, of course. In fact, I took the trouble to go outside and find a sharp stone with which to scratch "I forgive you" on the bonnet of the worship leader's car.'

Bible references: Leviticus 19:18; Proverbs 20:22; 24:29; Romans 12:17-21; 1 Corinthians 13:5.

Source: Adrian Plass, in *Deo*, Spring 1995.

106. Forgiveness

(Clergy, Death, Families, Heaven, History, Humour)

The eighteenth-century King of Prussia, Frederick William I, could not stand his brother-in-law, the English King George II. As Frederick William lay on his death bed in the year 1740, his Lutheran court chaplain urged him to ensure that his conscience was clear by forgiving all his enemies. This was the only way to make sure of his place in heaven.

'Are you certain?' asked the King.

'Absolutely,' answered the cleric.

'In that case,' said Frederick William to his wife, who was standing nearby, 'write to your brother and tell him that I forgive him, but be sure not to do it until after my death.'

Bible references: Matthew 6:12,14,15; 18:21-35; Mark 11:25; Luke 6:27-37; 11:4; 17:3-4; Ephesians 4:32; Colossians 3:13.

Source: Adapted from Geoffrey Regan, *Histrionics* (Robson Books, 1994), p 108.

107. Freedom

(Bondage, Conditioning, Human nature)

It's very easy to train a jumping flea. You simply place the flea in a jam jar and screw on the lid. As the flea jumps up, it will keep banging its head on the lid. After a while it will realise that this is not very enjoyable, and so will adjust the height of its jump so that it never quite reaches the top of the jam jar. After this, you can remove the lid, and the flea will stay in the jar. Even though the lid is no longer there, it will continue to believe in it.

Bible references: John 8:34; Romans 6:16-23; Galatians 3:22-3; 4:3-11; 2 Peter 2:19.

Source: Adapted from Adrian Hawkes, in *Breaking the Mould* (Kingsway, 1993), p 57.

108. Freedom

(Bondage, Conditioning, Fear, Holy Spirit, Human nature, Liberation)

Apparently it's equally simple to train an elephant. You find a sturdy tree stump and attach the elephant's leg to it by a strong chain. You then put some food just out of the elephant's reach, so that as it tries to get the food, the chain bites into its leg and inflicts pain. After a few days the elephant realises that to try and pull against the chain simply causes it pain, and isn't worth the effort. You can then exchange the chain for a rope. Although the elephant could easily snap the rope, it has now learned to accept its limitations, and will readily be restrained.

There is, however, one exception to this. Should a forest fire break out, and the flames approach the elephant, its fear of fire will outweigh its fear of pain. It will snap the rope, and if that happens, you will never again be able to train or condition it.

Bible references: Isaiah 61:1; Luke 4:18; John 8:31-6; Romans 6:16-23; 8:2, 15; 12:1-2; 2 Corinthians 3:17; Galatians 3:22-3; 4:3-7; 5:1, 13.

Source: Adapted from Adrian Hawkes, in *Breaking the Mould* (Kingsway, 1993), pp 59-60.

109. Grace
(Blindness, Conversion, Hymns, Jargon, Language, Modernity, Salvation, Sin, Humour)

As we enter the twenty-first century, people have trouble understanding and relating to the old-fashioned language of the church. So Doug Marlette has offered this rewritten version of one of our old-time hymns in the hope that it will make it more accessible to the modern worshipper.

Amazing grace, how sweet the sound,
That saved a stunted self-concept like me.
I once was stressed out, but now am empowered,
Was visually challenged, but now I see.

Bible references: John 1:14; Acts 15:11; Ephesians 2:4-8; 1 Timothy 1:14; Titus 2:11; 3:5-7.

Source: Quoted in David Wells, *No Place for Truth* (Eerdmans, 1993), p 137.

110. Obedience

(Faith, Fear, Fruitfulness, God, Holiness, Humility, Pride, Purity, Purpose, Sin)

Once upon a time there were six lumps of clay. They were destined to be made into flowerpots by the master potter on his wheel, fired in the kiln and then sold, hopefully to good homes.

But the first lump of clay said, 'I don't need any master potter. I'll make myself into a strong and attractive flowerpot: just you wait and see.' He's still trying.

The second lump said to the potter, 'I want to be really big and impressive: make me as big as you can.' The trouble was that he was only as big as all the other lumps, and so when he was finished he was very fragile, and broke before he was even fired.

The third lump of clay saw what had happened to her friend and laughed. 'I don't want to be bigger than I am,' she said. 'But I want to be beautiful. I want to be decorated with artistry and colour, covered in patterns and pictures. I'm meant to be more than just an ordinary, common or garden pot.' And so she was made beautiful, just as she had asked, but when she was finished she languished on the shelf. Nobody would buy her, for somehow she didn't look right as a simple flower pot, and yet she was hardly a work of art for the mantelpiece.

The fourth lump was made on the wheel, but was afraid to go into the kiln. 'It's so terribly hot in there!' she exclaimed. 'I'm sure I'd melt, or crack, or fall apart or something. Please don't put me in there!' And so she was left behind in the shed, and never again saw the light of day, let alone a garden.

The fifth lump wasn't frightened of the kiln, and went unconcernedly into the fire. Yet that was a big mistake, for this clay had not been properly purified. So as the temperature rose in the kiln, the intense heat sought out the faults and impurities deep within his being, cracked him wide open, and broke him in pieces. So he ended up in the dustbin.

And the sixth lump of clay? Why, she was happy to trust the potter and to go through whatever he thought, indeed knew, was best for her. As a result, she was a perfect specimen, and had a long and happy life doing exactly what she was meant to do: watching the flowers grow.

Bible references: Isaiah 29:16; 45:9; 64:8; Jeremiah 18:1-6; Romans 9:20-21; 2 Corinthians 4:7; 2 Timothy 2:20-21.

Source: Simon Coupland.

111. Running the race

(Cheating, Disqualification, Endurance, Heaven, Perseverance, Prize, Victory)

In 1980 a completely unknown athlete named Rosie Ruiz was the first woman to cross the line in the prestigious Boston Marathon. It was an amazing victory: nobody had ever heard of her before. But then somebody noticed her legs: they were flabby and out of condition. How could she possibly have run twenty-six miles? So then race officials started questioning spectators back along the course, and it turned out that nobody had seen Rosie Ruiz running. In fact she had joined the race in the last mile! She had fooled a few people for a short time, but all too quickly the true facts emerged. She was immediately disqualified and the winner's laurel wreath taken from her.

Bible references: Ecclesiastes 9:11; Acts 20:24; 1 Corinthians 9:24-7; Galatians 2:2; 5:7; Philippians 2:16; 3:12-14; 2 Timothy 2:5; 4:7; Hebrews 12:1.

Source: Adapted from Eugene Peterson, *The Quest* (Marshall Pickering, 1995), pp 106-7.

112. Service

(Bondage, Commitment, Freedom, Liberation, Servanthood)

In the days before the abolition of slavery in America, a fine negro slave was among the men being sold at auction. As the bidding began the negro noticed that a foreign-looking man was leading the bidding for him, consistently increasing his offer with every counter-bid. He began to shout and curse at the man, saying, 'If you buy me, I will never work for you. I'd sooner die than work for you. If you buy me, I'll try to kill you!' He knew that if he was bought by a foreign buyer, he'd be separated from his family and his relatives, and most likely never see them again.

But still the man went on bidding, and eventually the competitors gave in and the slave was sold to the foreign-looking stranger. He paid the money over to the auctioneer, received the bill of sale, and walked over to the slave. The crowd parted, waiting to see what would happen next. As the man reached the slave, he stretched out his hand with the bill of sale in it. 'Take it,' he said, 'You're a free man.'

The slave looked blank for a moment, then fell on his knees before this unknown benefactor. 'Sir,' he said, 'I will serve you and go with you wherever you want. Your home will be my home; your concerns my concerns, and your wish my command. I am yours.'

Bible references: Ruth 1:16-17; Matthew 20:26-7; Mark 10:43-4; John 8:35-6; Romans 6:16-23; 8:15; 1 Corinthians 7:22; 2 Corinthians 3:17; Galatians 4:3-9; 5:13; Ephesians 6:5-8; Colossians 3:22-4.

Source: Adapted from Peter Sertin, Paris 1981.

113. The Shepherd's voice

(Discernment, Guidance, Hearing God, Jesus, Names, Sheep, Voice of God)

A Western visitor to Israel was once out walking in the countryside when it became obvious that a heavy storm was about to break. As he took shelter, two shepherds joined him with their flocks, and he wondered how on earth the two men would disentangle the animals when they came to leave. He needn't have worried. Once the storm had passed, the two shepherds set off in different directions, each calling to his flock. The sheep ignored the call of the stranger and followed the sound of their own shepherd's voice. In no time at all the flocks had separated.

Bible references: Psalm 23; Isaiah 40:11; Ezekiel 34:11-16; Micah 5:4; Matthew 9:36; John 10:1-16, 27-9; Hebrews 13:20; 1 Peter 2:25; 5:4; Revelation 7:17.

Source: Adapted from Andy Arbuthnot in *Renewal*, August 1994.

114. To tell the truth ...

(Dishonesty, Goodness, Journalism, Lying, Media, Newspapers, Sin, Humour)

Lilian Carter, the mother of US President Jimmy Carter, was a formidable lady. She was once interviewed by a journalist from the deep south, who found it hard to believe that she had really lived such a morally upright life as people claimed. So the journalist asked 'Miss Lilian', as she was known, whether it was true that she had never told a lie, and that she had brought up little Jimmy not to tell one either. Miss Lilian thought hard, and then replied, 'No, I haven't consciously ever told a lie, and I never had to punish young Jimmy for having told one.'

'You mean,' pressed the reporter, 'that you never, *never* told a lie?'

'Well,' Miss Lilian admitted, 'I might have told a white lie on occasion.'

'Aha!' cried the journalist, seizing on this triumphantly. 'Can you give me an example?'

'Why, yes,' replied Miss Lilian. 'When you came through the door, I said I was glad to see you.'

Bible references: Leviticus 19:11; Zechariah 8:16; Ephesians 4:25; Colossians 3:9.

Source: Adapted from Sir Peter Ustinov, in *Durham First*, Spring 1995.

SIGNS AND WONDERS

115. Conviction

(Darkness, Grace, Hearing God, Holy Spirit, Light, Pictures, Power of God, Preaching, Prophecy, Repentance, Sin, Testimony, Vision)

It's the preacher's nightmare. You've worked hard to prepare your sermon. You're delivering it with enthusiasm and conviction. But the congregation don't seem to be on your wavelength. Eyes glaze over; heads begin to nod. This was exactly what happened to the young Jack Hayford on a wintry Sunday evening as he stood before a small congregation. And so, abandoning the sermon, he said almost despairingly, 'Let's pray.' He describes what happened next.

'I had no sooner closed my eyes when an indescribable blackness began to churn like a cloudy veil before my inner vision. I had never experienced anything like this before, and at the immediate moment did not realise I was having my first experience in receiving a 'word' – a prophetic picture. What I *did* realise was what this ugliness, this seething blackness represented: sin. It was plainly and awfully the grotesqueness of sin, sin in its suffocating power to blind, to swallow up, to

120

block the blessedness of the beauty of a soul's vision of God.

'I had only begun my prayer with the words, "Lord God, I pray that ..." when the vision burst over my awareness like a sudden storm. As it did, I could only begin to tremble with a sense of the horror of sin's blinding capability. So I paused, to gain composure, and then continued with the words "that you would help us see ..." Then it happened. The word exploded from my lips: "sin!" That single word rumbled up from out of my deepest being, breaking over my lips with a force that shocked me. I virtually bellowed it. Just once. But the effect was staggering to everyone present. Every head had snapped upward to look at me. Stunned amazement was written on every face. No one was asleep now!

'Looking into their wide-eyed countenances, an uncharacteristic boldness possessed me. I pointed straight at those in the pews and ordered, "Bow your heads!" Just as quickly as every head had snapped upwards to see what was happening to their young pastor, each head snapped back downwards in awed reverence before a power they felt in the room. I stepped from the platform and strode back and forth declaiming the horrendous nature of sin's blinding power and calling us to let God move on our hearts until his light would burn out any darkness.

'I hadn't spoken for two minutes when I gave directions. "I want every man to come to the altar area and pray. Each woman, turn and kneel where you are and call on the Lord". It was as though buttons had been punched in heaven, issuing electric jolts to everyone in the room. The people couldn't respond fast enough. The room was vibrating with aliveness. We prayed, repented, sang, praised God and read the Scriptures which the event brought to mind. It was glorious.

'If God had warned me in advance, I must confess that at that time in my ministry I probably would have been tempted to opt out. But as it occurred, it became not only a time of opening the door to God's grace in the life of that small congregation, it also became the beginning of my realising the purpose and power of the Holy Spirit's work of prophecy.'

Bible references: 1 Kings 8:28-30, 46-51; 2 Chronicles 7:14; Ezra 9:5-7; Nehemiah 1:4-11; Psalm 32:5; 38:18; 51; 106:6; Jeremiah 3:25; Daniel 9:3-19; John 16:8; Acts 26:18; Romans 13:12; 1 Corinthians 4:5; 1 Thessalonians 1:5; 1 John 1:5-2:2.

Source: Jack Hayford, *The Beauty of Spiritual Language*, quoted in *Renewal*, October 1993.

116. Healing – from dyslexia

(Angels, Children, Gifts of the Spirit, Holy Spirit, Miracles, Resting in the Spirit, Testimony, Vision)

Heather Harvey was thirteen when she went with a group from her church in Hopkinsville, Kentucky to the Airport Vineyard in Toronto. She had struggled with dyslexia throughout her school career, finding reading and writing difficult, and often having problems with understanding. In Toronto, she specifically asked for prayer for her learning disability, and as she was prayed for, she fell to the floor and lay very still.

Later she described what she had seen: the angels performing brain surgery on her! She heard God instructing them, and was told to be very still because 'this is very delicate surgery.' One of the angels got so excited that she began playing with Heather's brain, and God had to calm her down, saying, 'This is very serious, and not the time for play,' which Heather thought was funny. At the end, she saw herself praying for other friends with dyslexia.

Since that experience, reading is much easier for Heather; she doesn't make the characteristic mistakes such as reversing letters and missing the initial sound of words. She writes much more quickly and accurately, and is excited about learning, no longer confused and afraid. The first thing she did when she got home from Toronto was to pray for her eleven-year-old friend Monica, who was also dyslexic. Monica later told a story very similar to Heather's, how the angels shaved across her head, took the brain out, reshaped it, and sewed her back up. As with Heather, Monica's reading tutor subsequently said, 'No question, the dyslexia is gone.'

Bible references: Matthew 4:23; 8:16; 10:1, 8; 14:14; 15:30; Mark 1:33-4; 16:18; Luke 4:40; 5:15, 17; 6:17-19; 9:2, 6; 10:9; John 5:14-15; Acts 10:38; 1 Corinthians 12:9, 28.

Source: Adapted from Guy Chevreau, *Catch the Fire* (Marshall Pickering, 1994), pp 171-3.

117. Healing – a misunderstanding

(Disability, Miracles, Nuns, Pope, Vatican, Wheelchair, Humour)

In 1984, Dr Jan Lavric from Clayton, near Doncaster, had helped to organise a pilgrimage to Rome for a group of disabled people. The highlight of the trip was an audience with the Pope in the Vatican, and by the time Dr Clayton had seen to the needs of the disabled members of the party, there was just one empty seat left: a wheelchair. But no sooner had he sat down than a nun wheeled him off to be blessed by the Pope. Dr Lavric had no chance to explain; the Pope said the words of blessing, then left the room. As Dr Lavric got up from his seat, there was a tremendous commotion among the nuns. They naturally thought it was a miracle!

Source: *The Times*, 2 May 1984.

118. Healing – three blind men

(Bible, Blindness, Differences, Jesus, Miracles, Testimony, Humour)

It so happened that three men who had been blind but who had been cured by Jesus all met up in Jerusalem, and naturally they started talking about their experiences. 'Wasn't Jesus amazing?' said the first. 'The way he made the mud and put it on your eyes – I mean, why didn't anyone else think of doing that before?'

'What do you mean, made mud?' asked the second. 'Jesus didn't make mud! It was just his saliva. He spat on my eyelids and put his hands on them and then I could see. I admit it wasn't very clear at first....'

'It *was* mud, I tell you,' replied the first. People told me afterwards. He spat on the ground, then he put the mud on my eyelids, and then I had to go and wash in the Pool of Siloam.'

'Wash in a pool?' echoed the second man. 'You had to wash in a pool? This is the same Jesus we're talking about, is it? I didn't have to wash in a pool. As soon as he put his hands on my eyes the second time, I could see clearly.'

Now it was the turn of the first man to sound sceptical. 'Why did he have to touch you the second time?' he asked. 'Didn't it work the first time?'

'Well, yes and no,' came the reply. 'I could see, but it was all blurred, fuzzy – people looked a bit like trees walking about. Then the second time it was clear as day. Why, did you see straightaway?'

'As soon as I washed in the pool, like I told you,' said the first man. 'I can't understand why you didn't have to wash in a pool. I'm not sure yours was a proper cure. I mean, you didn't wash, you didn't see properly the first time – it all sounds a bit dodgy to me.'

'What do you mean, dodgy?' retorted the other man. 'Jesus didn't need to send me to some pool for cleansing. He didn't need to make mud for my eyes. I expect it was because you were such a sinner that he had to go to all those lengths to heal you!'

'Hark who's talking!' shouted the first, and the argument was just getting heated when the third man spoke up for the first time. 'You're both as bad as each other!' he said. 'I tell you, when Jesus cured me, he didn't use spit and he didn't use mud and I didn't have to wash and it happened all at once. He just said, "Receive your sight; your faith has healed you," and I could see – just like that. If it really was Jesus who cured you – and I'm beginning to have my doubts – it's pretty obvious that you both had very weird experiences. If I were you, I'd keep quiet, or people might get the wrong idea about you.'

And that sparked off a furious row which was evidently going to run and run....

Bible references: Matthew 20:29-34; Mark 8:22-6; 10:46-52; Luke 18:35-43; John 9:1-41.

Source: Adapted from Michael Rees, Cambridge 1979.

119. Healing – under persecution

(Children, Conversion, Faith, Families, Gifts of the Spirit, Miracles, Suffering, Testimony, Witness)

Pastor Peterson Sozi was a leader in the Ugandan church during the dreadful years of Idi Amin's reign in the 1970s, when services had to be held in secret in the face of persecution. One woman who attended these secret meetings brought her twelve-year-old handicapped son, and when Sozi prayed for him, God miraculously healed the boy. To the delight of everybody present, he started to run around the room in exuberant joy.

However, the mother's joy was tempered by her concern about how the boy's father would take the news. For he was a member of Amin's notorious State Research Bureau, the secret police, and she had often heard him boast of how he had personally killed so-called enemies of the regime, tossing their bodies into the forest or the river Nile. But there was no concealing what had happened: they could only pray.

When the father saw his son, he demanded to know what had happened, and who had healed the boy. In fear and trembling, his wife replied, 'These are the people that you are persecuting. They are the ones who did this.' To her amazement and relief, the father began attending church services with her, and in time, invited some of his colleagues in the State Research Bureau. Many of them went on to become Christians through Sozi's ministry.

Bible references: Matthew 9:18-25; 15:21-8; 17:14-18; Mark 5:22-43; 7:24-30; 9:17-27; Luke 8:41-56; 9:38-42; John 4:47-53; Acts 9:3-5; 22:7-8; 26:14-15.

Source: Adapted from *Renewal*, February 1995.

120. Listening

(Gifts of the Spirit, Holy Spirit, Prophecy, Silence, Tongues, Worship)

Andy and Audrey Arbuthnot went on a trip to Uganda where they witnessed the Holy Spirit working in wonderful ways. However, there were times when they wished people would be a little more sensitive to the Spirit's work.

When we invited the Holy Spirit to come down and the noisy exuberance was released, it seemed wrong for us to try to quench it. However, after about twenty minutes of uproar, Audrey and I each held out a hand and we started praying quietly, asking the Lord to bring his peace. Within a few minutes the tumult had ceased.

Still, however, a handful of individuals almost seemed carried away in a form of ecstasy, shouting and waving their arms. They were now becoming a disturbance to those around them. With one woman in particular, I had considerable difficulty in stopping her wild shouting in tongues and her gesticulations. Was I on the wrong lines to stop her, I wondered? We were with people of a very different culture and who were much more exuberant in temperament than we are in England. However, having helped her to stop shouting, I was relieved and encouraged to notice five minutes later that, as she now lifted her face to heaven in complete silence, she was obviously basking in the light of the Holy Spirit.

I remember a charismatic conference in England where there was much shouting of 'Alleluia' and praising loudly in tongues. The only word which seemed to us to come from the Lord was when someone spoke, 'My children, I long for you to listen to me.' But nobody listened. They were much too busy shouting praises.

Bible references: 1 Samuel 3:1-10; 1 Kings 19:11-12; Psalm 46:10; 1 Corinthians 14:1-20, 26-33.

Source: Andy Arbuthnot, in *Renewal*, December 1993.

121. Miracle

(Answers to prayer, Children, Families, Infertility, Mothers, Prayer, Purpose, Suffering, Testimony)

Five years after Celia Bowring's marriage, the news was broken to her and her husband Lyndon that, as far as medical science was concerned, they would always remain childless. It was a bitter blow, and the disappointment, pain and resentment that they felt made it the lowest point of their lives. They tried praying for a miracle, but nothing seemed to happen. Until one day Celia was pleading with God yet again to give her the longed-for baby, when suddenly he seemed to answer, 'Yes, if that is what you really want, instead of the plans and purposes I have outlined for you.'

At that moment Celia realised that she had been so obsessed with this desperate desire for motherhood that she was missing out on the other blessings which God was actually giving her but which she was too preoccupied to appreciate. So she responded, 'No, of course not, Lord; it's your best that I want.' Deep down inside something changed. It didn't become easy to visit friends in maternity wards or to walk past Mothercare, but she had reached a place of acceptance, the certainty that God was in all this somehow.

Some years later when they were helping to lead Spring Harvest seminars about marriage, Lyndon courageously shared the burden of their childlessness. Many people responded to his openness and honesty by praying for them, as so many had prayed for them before. Yet to their surprise and delight, and their complete confusion about God's will, their first child, Daniel, was born a year and a half later! Not only that, but two more children followed. Celia says, 'It was a miracle – as God responded to the prayers of those who loved us and even people who had never met us. But we knew it was not our desires but God's time and plan that had made this happen.

'But how about all the couples who pray but no baby comes? It cannot be understood; the mysteries about God are all unfathomable.... and yet one simple miraculous truth is certain: that he loves us. Any way he chooses to deal with us is in the light of his perfect love. But it takes a tough decision of the will for each of us to believe it, for when suffering comes we can rarely see how or why it can possibly be his best for us.'

Bible references: Genesis 11:30; 17:15-19; 18:9-15; 21:1-3; 25:21; 29:31; 30:22-3; Judges 13:2-24; 1 Samuel 1:2-20; Psalm 113:9; Isaiah 54:1; Luke 1:7-25.

Source: Adapted from *Renewal*, November 1993.

122. Peace

(Answers to prayer, Church, Faith, God, Persecution, Prayer, Sovereignty of God, War)

The Bible speaks of the day when swords will be hammered into ploughshares, and from the former Soviet Union comes the true story of a former missile silo which was used to build a place of worship.

Baptists in Kobryn were given permission by the Byelorussian authorities to erect their first officially sanctioned meeting place since the congregation was formed in 1925. The problem was that they were desperately short of building materials for the new church, so they were allowed to demolish a disused barracks and missile silo which were situated nearby. They salvaged bricks, concrete blocks and steel, and it was while they were knocking down a brick wall that they came across an empty artillery shell sealed into the wall. The shell had been used as a sort of time capsule when the complex was under construction forty-two years earlier, and it revealed the source of the bricks. A letter inside it said, 'These bricks came from Polish Orthodox and Russian Orthodox churches. If the complex is ever torn down, we ask that the bricks be used to build churches.'

The churches had been destroyed under Joseph Stalin, when to be a Christian meant to face persecution; in those dark days, it would have been unthinkable for the construction workers' request to be granted. Now, quite remarkably, the authorities had answered their prayer.

Bible references: Psalm 46:9; Isaiah 2:4; 9:5-7; Jeremiah 30:10; Hosea 2:18; Micah 4:3-4; Zechariah 9:10.

Source: Adapted from *Renewal*, May 1993.

123. Pictures

(Evangelism, Gifts of the Spirit, Guidance, Hearing God, Holy Spirit, Language, Listening, Mission, Prayer, Prophecy, Testimony, Vision, Voice of God)

Rob Warner, the pastoral leader of Herne Hill Baptist Church, felt that God had given him a picture. It was just a picture without an interpretation, so he wasn't sure about sharing it. What was more, the service had already finished, and people were starting to drift away. But God seemed to be prompting him, so in a low-key way, he told the rest of the congregation what he had seen.

'There's a walled courtyard with more walls beyond, and beyond that there's a river. Jesus says he will take you past the walls and he will be the bridge over the river into the land he has prepared for you.' The meaning of the picture remained unclear. What was God trying to say through it? Was it perhaps to do with a rebuilding project the church was thinking of undertaking?

The following Thursday, Rob attended an Ichthus leaders' meeting, and during the praise and prayer time a visitor from Germany stood up and began to speak – in German. As he spoke, a Swiss Ichthus worker who was there provided a simultaneous translation. The visitor began by thanking God for the gift of prophecy, then shared a picture which he believed was from God.

'There are walls before you.' Rob Warner wondered whether this had anything to do with the walls which he had seen in his picture. 'Beyond the walls there's a river.' He sat up with a start! 'Jesus will take you beyond the walls and he will be the bridge for you into the land he has prepared for you.' By now, Rob Warner says, 'I was on the edge of my seat, wide-eyed and lost for words. My picture was being repeated almost word for word, translated from another language and given by someone I'd never met before.'

The German guest then added a final detail which Rob had not been given. 'And the Lord says your church is to go to the Muslim peoples.' Now unbeknown to anyone in Ichthus, one of Rob's close colleagues, Mike Wheate, was due to fly out to Egypt the very next day, to explore the possibility of working there with Operation Mobilisation. Less than four weeks later he confirmed that he would indeed be going.

Rob Warner comments, 'Did we need the picture to obey God? No. I'm sure those involved would have obeyed God's calling anyway. But it demonstrates the Spirit's commitment to evangelism in a dramatic and memorable way. It also shows how keen God is to speak to us, and the way spiritual gifts cross national boundaries when the people of God are open to the Spirit. And it will certainly encourage speaking out with boldness the next time God gives one of us a picture!'

Bible references: Genesis 15:1; Numbers 12:6; Daniel 1:17; 2:19-23; Amos 7:1-9; 8:1-2; Acts 10:9-17; 16:9-10.

Source: Adapted from *Renewal*, October 1991.

124. Pictures

(Bible, Gifts of the Spirit, Guidance, Hearing God, Holy Spirit, Listening, Prayer, Vision, Voice of God, Humour)

James Ryle tells how he was staying in a neighbouring city before leading a training seminar. He was just settling down to sleep when he sensed that God wanted to tell him something. He asked the Lord what it was, and saw a picture of a road sign with a little pink pig standing in the grass beside it. He asked the Lord what this might mean, and when no answer was immediately forthcoming, began to speculate.

'I thought perhaps the Lord was trying to tell me there would be demons in the meeting tomorrow, and I was to cast them into pigs (Mt 8:31-2); or perhaps the people would be like pigs that went back to wallow in the mud after they were cleansed (2 Pet 2:22); or maybe I shouldn't even teach because it would be like casting my pearls before swine (Mt 7:6). I even thought he might be telling me not to look at any pretty girls who were there, because they would be like a gold ring in a pig's nose (Prov 11:22)! But I could not come up with anything that made sense out of this strange vision.'

In the end he again asked God what he was trying to say to him, and the Lord answered, 'James, did you read the road sign?' 'Lord, I'm sorry,' he replied, 'I was so taken by the pig that I didn't even look at the sign. What did it say?' When the Lord showed him the picture again, on the sign was written: 'Don't Be Distracted!' Then the Lord spoke to him again, 'I am speaking to my people in "road signs" all the time, but they are so distracted by the little pigs that they seldom notice what I am saying.'

Bible references: Genesis 15:1; 46:2; Numbers 12:6; 1 Samuel 3:1-10; 1 Kings 19:11-13; Proverbs 11:22; Daniel 1:17; 2:19-23; Amos 7:1-9; 8:1-2; Matthew 1:20-1; 2:13, 19, 22; 7:6; 8:31-2; Acts 9:10-16; 10:9-17; 16:9-10; 18:9-10; 2 Peter 2:22.

Source: Adapted from James Ryle, *Hippo in the Garden* (Highland, 1992), pp 44-5.

125. Resting in the Spirit

(Gifts of the Spirit, Holy Spirit, Humility, Ministry, Peace, Prayer, Relaxation, Testimony)

R. T. Kendall is senior pastor at Westminster Chapel, and a

highly respected Bible teacher and preacher. He was at first sceptical of the move of the Holy Spirit associated with the Toronto Airport Vineyard, but having talked to friends whom he respected at Holy Trinity Brompton, he invited the vicar, Sandy Millar, to bring a team to Westminster Chapel to address and pray for the deacons and their wives. He had previously been prayed for, when, as he says, 'Nothing happened. My wife joined us as they were praying for me. After about two minutes she was on the floor. I had never seen such a radiant smile on her face. She wept, she laughed, and she said to me later that if this was what being slain in the Spirit was, she could see why people wanted it.

'Then, on the evening when Sandy Millar and his staff came to our church, we were about to go home when one of them asked if he could pray for me. I said, "Sure, but I must tell you I've been prayed for many times." I didn't want him to get his hopes up. Within a minute or so, suddenly my mind became so relaxed. The nearest I can think of to describe it was when I had sodium pentathol years ago when I had major surgery. Yet I wasn't unconscious. I felt myself falling forward.

'For me, it was so humbling. I think God was wanting to teach me to be humbled, to look stupid and to be a fool. There I was on the floor in front of all my deacons and their wives. I was embarrassed. I think that was what God wanted to do to me.'

Bible references: Jeremiah 23:9; Daniel 8:18; 10:8-9, 17; Revelation 1:17.

Source: Adapted from *Renewal*, October 1994.

126. Tongues

(Church, Clergy, Fear, Gifts of the Spirit, Hearing God, Holy Spirit, Humility, Listening, Pride, Risks, Voice of God)

At St Aldate's in Oxford in 1993, a young man came to the front and said he felt he had a message in tongues to share. The rector, David MacInnes, admitted afterwards, 'I didn't want a tongue. I thought it might make us look a little odd because there were a number of visiting professors from Harvard. I had about thirty seconds in which to decide what to do.'

He explained to the congregation that someone was about to speak in another language, which although it might be unfamiliar to those who were listening was a prayer language, identified in the New Testament as a wonderful gift from God. Then the man spoke, and David MacInnes cringed because he went on so long. When the tongue eventually came to an end, he asked whether anyone had an interpretation, and was encouraged when a mature member of the congregation, a man with hesitations about the gifts of the Spirit, answered that he felt he had something to say.

He gave what appeared to be half of a message, which broke off rather abruptly, and said that he had no more, but knew there was more to come. Then David MacInnes noticed a Japanese woman in the congregation who had only been coming a few months. She was clearly uncertain about coming forward. He called her up and she proceeded to repeat what had already been said, and to complete it. It was, as David MacInnes comments, 'a very clear message to the church, which left no one in any doubt that it was from God. People admitted it opened new horizons for them.'

Bible references: Mark 16:17; Acts 2:4; 1 Corinthians 12:10; 14:1-33.

Source: Adapted from *Renewal*, August 1993.

127. Tongues

(Gifts of the Spirit, Holy Spirit, Meditation, Peace, Prayer, Psychology, Relaxation, Resting in the Spirit, Testimony, Zen)

As part of his training to become a clinical psychologist, Dan Montgomery was hooked up to sophisticated equipment which measured muscle tension and brain-wave patterns. The baseline readings at the start of the experiment showed a fair degree of stress (beta brain waves and 120 micro volts of upper torso muscle tension, for those who understand such things!). This wasn't surprising – he had had a hard day. 'I'll be back in ten minutes,' said the researcher. 'Do whatever you can to relax and then we'll take a new reading.'

Dan decided to use the time to pray silently in tongues. When the researcher returned, he banged the machine with his hand and scratched his head. Then he shrugged his shoulders and wrote down the readings (theta brain waves and five micro volts of upper body muscle tension). Dan asked what it was that had so surprised him. He didn't reply directly, but asked, 'Have you had years of relaxation training?' 'No,' was the honest answer. 'Well,' he said, 'I don't know how to account for it, but your body and mind were as serene as a Zen monk who's meditated for twenty years!'

Dan concluded, 'Praying in tongues brings relaxation and serenity.'

Bible references: Mark 16:17; Acts 10:46; 19:6; Romans 8:26-7; 1 Corinthians 12:10; 14:2, 4, 18; Ephesians 6:18.

Source: Adapted from *Renewal*, September 1994.

THE HUMAN CONDITION

128. Alienation

(Despair, God, Human nature, Life, Literature, Loneliness, Pessimism, Providence, Silence of God, Suffering, Unbelief, the World)

One literary critic summed up the writings of the playwright Samuel Beckett as follows:

> All Beckett's writing is haunted by the feeling most of us have experienced, but fortunately only rarely and not usually for long: the feeling that we are totally alone in the world, unprotected by higher beings, and not deserted only because we have never really been accompanied; that our past is inexplicable and our future unknowable, and that the dingy body we inhabit is probably all there is. It would be unendurable if it were not so grotesquely laughable, no? To anyone who has ever felt this, a voice that can speak coherently about such things is a consolation and a reassurance: the voice of another orphan.

Bible references: Genesis 2:18; Job 7:16; Psalm 14:1;

42:3, 10; 53:1; Ecclesiastes 1:2-18; 2:17-23; 3:11; 12:8.

Source: the *Sunday Times*, 30 December 1989.

129. Animals

(Creation, God, History, Human nature, Humour)

Our forebears believed that God had ordered the whole of creation for the express benefit of mankind. Thus the Tudors and Stuarts thought that he had designed apes and parrots for our amusement; songbirds to entertain us; the louse to make us keep ourselves clean, and horseflies 'that men should exercise their wit and industry to guard themselves against them.' The lobster served several purposes at once, providing food in the shape of its flesh, exercise in the need to crack it open, and instruction in the form of its remarkable suit of armour.

Perhaps the most incredible piece of lateral thinking was the view of physician George Cheyne that 'the Creator made horse's excrement smell sweet, because he knew that men would often be in its vicinity'!

Bible references: Genesis 1:26-8; 2:19-20; 9:2-3; Psalm 8:6-8; 115:16.

Source: Adapted from Keith Thomas, *Man and the Natural World*, quoted in Tim Cooper, *Green Christianity* (Spire, 1990), pp 49-50.

130. Birth

(Children, Dishonesty, Families, Grandmothers, Life, Lying, Mothers, School, Truth, Humour)

A little boy had to write an essay on birth for school, so he asked his mother, 'Mum, how was I born?' 'Well, dear,' she answered, somewhat hesitantly, 'When we decided that we wanted a little baby, we asked God for one, and a stork brought you through the air and left you on our doorstep.' Then he went to his grandmother and asked, 'Grandma, how was Mummy born?' Grandma, too, looked rather embarrassed, and after a bit of umming and erring said, 'Well, when your Grandpa and I wanted to have a baby, we asked God for one, and next morning, when we looked out in the garden, there was your mother, a little baby lying underneath the gooseberry bush.' 'And what about you, Grandma?' the child persisted, 'Were you born in the same way?' 'That's right, dear,' she said, 'I was.' 'I see,' the lad replied. Then he went off and started to write: 'In the last three generations there have not been any natural births in our family.'

Bible references: John 1:12-13; 3:3-7; Titus 3:5; James 1:18; 1 Peter 1:23.

Source: Adapted from David Watson, Cambridge 1979.

131. Despair

(Alcohol, Death, Drugs, Life, Modern life, Prison, Suicide, Young people)

At 4.15 pm on Saturday 19 February 1983, the station

sergeant at Maidstone police station made a routine check on cell number one, where twenty-one-year-old Olivier Clairmonte had been placed an hour earlier. He found him hanging by his underpants from a wall bracket.

Olly, as his friends knew him, had been in a scuffle with some security guards at a local shopping centre, and had head-butted a policeman during his arrest. Not a major crime. But it was not Olly's first time in a cell: he had hit a policeman once before and had served three months in a detention centre for young offenders. When he came out, he had vowed to his father that he would rather kill himself than spend another night in a prison cell.

One of Olly's close circle of friends, Adrian, had already killed himself just before Christmas by jumping off a building. 'He might have been doing it for the crack,' said a friend, 'thinking he'd walk away from it.' Another of Adrian's friends was Rat, who described himself as 'Olly's best living friend'. He talked about how it feels to be young and unemployed, with little money and even less hope. 'We're rock-and-roll suicides,' he said. 'We've all been into so much glue, drugs, drink and enjoying ourselves, that in the end it's suicide, whether by accident or on purpose. I know I'm not going to survive another three years. I've had a laugh in my own way – and when I die I'll go in my own way, not on purpose, but because everything is just too much.'

Bible references: Ecclesiastes 1:2-11; 2:10-11; 4:2-3; 12:8; Ephesians 2:1-3.

Source: Adapted from the *Sunday Times*, 20 March 1983.

132. Evolution

(Creation, Faith, God, Life, Science)

It is one of the myths of modern society that scientific knowledge and faith in God are mutually exclusive. The astronomer Professor Chandra Wickramasinghe wrote the following in a letter to the *Times*:

> The idea that life was put together by random shuffling of constituent molecules can be shown (in the words of Sir Fred Hoyle) to be as ridiculous and improbable as the proposition that a tornado blowing through a junk yard may assemble a Boeing 747. The aircraft had a creator and so might life. The possibility that life had a cosmic genetic engineer for a creator, one that emerged naturally according to the laws of physics within the Universe, is a logical option that cannot be lightly dismissed.

Bible references: Genesis 1; Job 38; Psalm 8:3; 19:1-6; 104; Isaiah 40:12-20; Jeremiah 51:15-16; John 1:3; Acts 14:15; 17:24; Romans 1:20; 1 Corinthians 8:6; Colossians 1:16.

Source: Quoted in *The Lion Handbook of Christian Belief* (Lion, 1982), p 216.

133. Experience

(Despair, Disillusionment, Fame, Life, Success, Water, the World)

Lord Byron enjoyed life to the full, but as he looked back

over the years, he wrote: 'Drank every cup of joy, heard every
trump of fame; drank early; deeply drank; drank draughts
which common millions might have drunk. Then died of
thirst, because there was no more to drink.'

Bible references: Ecclesiastes 1:12-2:23.

Source: Quoted in Richard Bewes, *The Church Overcomes*
(Mowbray, 1984), p 90.

134. Food

*(Alcohol,   Consumption,   Human   nature,   Modern   life,
Nutrition)*

By the time we reach seventy, the average person will have
eaten three cows, seventeen pigs, twenty-five lambs, 420
chickens, four miles of sausages, 1,190 portions of fish and
chips, 3,500 loaves of bread and 2,240 bags of crisps,
according to a survey compiled with the help of the Ministry
of Agriculture and the British Nutrition Foundation. To wash
this down we will have swallowed the equivalent of sixty
bathfulls of milk and 93,000 cups of tea, together with 910
gallons of beer, 25,000 glasses of wine and 7,280 measures of
spirits.

Bible references: Psalm 104:15, 27-28; Matthew 5:25-6;
6:11; Luke 11:3; 12:22-4; John 6:27, 33-5; Acts 14:17; 1
Timothy 6:17.

Source: Quoted in the *Daily Telegraph*, 1984.

135. Human nature

(Creation, Life, Science)

Man is nothing but fat enough for seven bars of soap;
iron enough for one medium-sized nail;
sugar enough for seven cups of tea;
lime enough to whitewash one chicken coop;
phosphorous enough to tip 2,200 matches;
magnesium enough for one dose of salts;
potash enough to explode one toy cannon;
sulphur enough to rid one dog of fleas.

Bible references: Job 7:17-18; Psalm 8:4-8; 144:3-4;
Hebrews 2:6.

Source: Professor C.E.M. Joad, quoted in *Dancing in the Dark?*, Spring Harvest notes for 1994 (Lynx Communications, 1994), p 20.

136. Loneliness

(Alcohol, Death, Despair, Disillusionment, Drugs, Friendship, Human nature, Life, Lifestyle, Money, Suicide, Wealth)

In 1994 a British expatriate died in Los Angeles after taking a cocktail of alcohol and pain-killing drugs. A friend of his in the high-living local jet set commented, 'The quantity of life here is high, but the quality of life is low. Nobody will love you when you are down, you have to cope on your own. There is an LA saying, "Your best friend is your dog." '

Bible references: Job 15:27-33; 27:16-23; Psalm 39:6; 49; 73:2-20; Ecclesiastes 2:17-23; 3:18-21; Matthew 6:19-21; Luke 12:13-20; 16:19-31.

Source: Quoted in the *Daily Telegraph*, 8 October 1994.

137. Modernity

(End times, Eschatology, False prophets, History, Human nature, Optimism, Pride, Religion, Technology)

On 1 May 1851, Queen Victoria opened the Great Exhibition at the Crystal Palace in London's Hyde Park. To judge by the description of it in her diary, she found it a spiritual experience. It 'was magical; so vast, so glorious, so touching. One felt – as so many did whom I have since spoken to – filled with devotion, more so than by any service I have ever heard.' The queen also noted that she saw the exhibition as a '"peace festival" which united the industry of all nations of the earth.'

The *Times* in its report next morning similarly drew on religious imagery, describing the soaring glass palace as 'far more lofty and spacious than the vaults of even our noblest cathedrals'. In an echo of 1 Corinthians 2:9, the magnificence of the spectacle suggested to the writer 'something even more than sense could scan, or imagination attain'. Like the queen, the paper also concluded on a visionary note, comparing the exhibition with 'that day when all ages and climes shall be gathered round that Throne of their Maker.'

This misplaced eschatological optimism reflected the sentiments of Prince Albert, who had organised the exhibition and opened it. In his public speech he declared, 'Nobody who has paid any attention to the peculiar features of our present era will doubt for a moment that we are living at a period of most wonderful transition, which tends rapidly to accomplish that great end to which indeed all history points – the realisation of the unity of mankind.'

Bible references: Genesis 11:3-4; 1 Corinthians 2:9.

Source: Quoted in J. Richard Middleton and Brian J. Walsh, *Truth is Stranger than it Used to Be* (SPCK, 1995), pp 18-19.

138. Sabbath

(Commandments, Human nature, Relaxation, War, Work)

During the Second World War, a group of loyal factory workers decided to give up their Sunday rest day and continue working in order to increase output. In fact, production fell, proving that the way in which we are made requires rest and recreation for one day out of seven.

Bible references: Genesis 2:2-3; Exodus 20:8-11; 23:12; 31:12-17; 34:21; Deuteronomy 5:12-15; Nehemiah 13:15-22; Jeremiah 17:19-22; Amos 8:5; Mark 2:27.

Source: Adapted from Tony Wilmot, Paris, 9 September 1979.

139. Technology

(Accidents, Human nature, God, Modernity, Optimism, Pride, Salvation, Shipwreck, Sin)

The *Titanic* was said to be unsinkable, and people truly believed it. On 10 April 1912, as the passengers embarked on the liner's maiden voyage, one of the crew said to a lady who expressed her nervousness, 'Madam, even God himself could not sink this ship.' But then the unthinkable happened – 500 miles south of Newfoundland the liner struck a huge iceberg, tearing a hole 300 feet long in her side. As the icy water flooded into her heart and the ship began to list, one passenger was heard to say, 'Why doesn't the captain press a button and make it all right again?'

Bible references: Psalm 20:7; Proverbs 16:18; Isaiah 14:12-15; 31:1-3; Ezekiel 28:2; Luke 12:16-21; James 4:13-16.

Source: Adapted from *Headlines*, issue 1.

140. Woman

(Church, Cross-dressing, Discrimination, History, War)

In 1782, Deborah Sampson, a Baptist from Massachusetts, dressed as a man to enlist in the Continental army and fight in the American War of Independence against the British. As Private Robert Shurtliff, she was wounded twice in the fighting, but her true identity remained undiscovered for over a year. When the war was over, she married and bore three children, eventually receiving due recognition of her military service and an army pension. Her church was less sympathetic: they excommunicated her for impersonating a man.

Bible references: Deuteronomy 22:5.

Source: Adapted from *Christian History*, issue 50.

SUFFERING AND EVIL

141. The Antichrist

(End times, Eschatology, Evil, Prophecy, Revelation, Second Coming)

In 1981, a woman called Mary Stewart Relfe wrote a book called 'When Your Money Fails ... The 666 System is Here,' in which she produced all sorts of evidence to show that the 'number of the beast' (Rev 13:18) is being insidiously foisted upon the American people by the agents of the antichrist.

Relfe's researches convinced her that Olivetti, Lear Seigler and National Cash Register computer systems, brands of work gloves, fertiliser, shirts, and spare parts for caterpillar tractors all used 666 in their product codes. The three giants of discount shopping, Sears, Montgomery Ward and JC Penny all used computer programs with 666 as a prefix, as did the World Bank, Medicaid, and the recruiting arm of the United States Army. Relfe even came across a children's mathematics book called '666 Jellybeans', proving to her that the conspiracy was already corrupting the next generation.

Bible references: Revelation 13:11-18.

Source: Adapted from the *Sunday Times*, 5 December 1982.

142. Brokenness

(Failure, Faith, Light, Love, Pain, Suffering)

The opal is a stone with a broken heart. It is full of minute fissures that allow air inside, and that air refracts the light. That is how the stone acquires its characteristic lustre – through its brokenness. A flawless opal would have no radiance, no warmth, no colour.

But if the opal is kept in a cold, dark place, it will lose its lustre. What it needs is warmth – such as the warmth of a human hand – and light to shine on it. Only then will its glory be revealed.

Bible references: Romans 8:17-25; 2 Corinthians 1:3-11; 4:7-12; 12:7-10; 13:4; Philippians 3:10-11; Colossians 1:24; Hebrews 5:8; 1 Peter 4:12-13, 19.

Source: Adapted from Barbara Johnson, *Splashes of Joy in the Cesspools of Life* (Word, 1992), p 80.

143. Cruelty

(Conditioning, Evil, Experimentation, Human nature, Pain, Science, Suffering, Torture)

In the 1960s, Stanley Milgram showed how far people would

go in inflicting pain on others as long as somebody else took responsibility for it. The subjects involved in the experiment were asked to give electric shocks to students whom they could see through a one-way mirror. The students didn't actually receive a shock, but acted as if they had done, jerking and writhing as if in pain. By way of explanation, the volunteer torturers were told how the students would learn much more quickly if they were 'shocked' hard enough whenever they gave a wrong answer. Within a few minutes, some subjects were giving what they thought were shocks of as much as 450 volts! They were so caught up in the experiment that they never stopped to think of the sheer cruelty of what they were doing.

Bible references: Genesis 6:5; 8:21; Jeremiah 17:9; Matthew 15:19; Mark 7:21-2; John 2:24-5; Galatians 5:19-21.

Source: Adapted from John White and Ken Blue, *Healing the Wounded* (IVP, 1985), p 49.

144. Demons

(The Devil, Evil, God, Hallowe'en)

The writer Anthony Burgess once wrote in a column in the *Evening Standard*:

Having lived in Borneo for several years, where the omnipresent jungle breeds belief in demons, I am forced to an acceptance of the existence of malevolent powers in the world of the spirit. Even to enact the childish rites of Hallowe'en is to touch the fringe of another world. And if evil exists in this other world it is more than likely that good exists too.

Bible references: Matthew 4:24; 8:16, 28-34; 9:32-3; 10:1, 8; 12:22-9; 15:21-8; 17:14-18; Mark 1:23-7, 32-4, 39; 3:11-15, 22-7; 5:1-20; 6:7; 7:24-30; 9:17-27; 16:17; Luke 4:33-6; 4:41; 8:26-39; 9:1; 10:17-20; 11:14-26; Acts 5:16; 8:7; 16:18; 19:13-16.

Source: *Idea.*

145. Demons

(The Devil, Evil, Exorcism, Medicine, Possession, Psychology, Science)

'In common with 99 per cent of psychiatrists and the majority of clergy, I did not think the devil existed. Still, priding myself on being an open-minded scientist, I felt I had to examine the evidence that might challenge my inclination in the matter. It occurred to me that if I could see one good old-fashioned case of possession I might change my mind....

'So I decided to go out and look for a case. I wrote around and let it be known that I was interested in observing cases of purported possession for evaluation. Referrals trickled in. The first two cases turned out to be suffering from standard psychiatric disorders, as I had suspected, and I began making marks on my scientific pistol.

'The third case turned out to be the real thing.

'Since then I have also been deeply involved with another case of genuine possession. In both cases I was privileged to be present at their successful exorcisms. The vast majority of cases described in the literature are those of possession by minor demons. These two were highly unusual in that both were cases of Satanic possession. I now know Satan is real. I have met it.'

Bible references: Matthew 4:24; 8:16, 28-34; 9:32-3; 10:1, 8; 12:22-9; 15:21-8; 17:14-18; Mark 1:23-7, 32-4, 39; 3:11-15, 22-7; 5:1-20; 6:7; 7:24-30; 9:17-27; 16:17; Luke 4:33-6, 41; 8:26-39; 9:1; 10:17-20; 11:14-26; Acts 5:16; 8:7; 16:18; 19:13-16.

Source: M. Scott Peck, *People of the Lie* (Rider Books, 1988), pp 182-3.

146. Forgiveness

(Children, Concentration camps, Evil, God, Holocaust, Jews, Mercy, Murder, Nazism, Second World War, Suffering)

The American writer Elie Wiesel, winner of the Nobel Peace Prize in 1986, who was in Auschwitz as a child, spoke at the unofficial commemoration marking the fiftieth anniversary of the camp's liberation on 27 January 1945.

Although we know that God is merciful, please God do not have mercy on those who have created this place. God of forgiveness, do not forgive those murderers of Jewish children here. Do not forgive the murderers and their accomplices.

Those who have been here remember the nocturnal processions of children and more children and more children, frightened, quiet, so quiet and so beautiful. If we could simply look at one, our heart would break. Did it not break the heart of the murderers? God, merciful God, do not have mercy on those who had no mercy on Jewish children.

Bible references: Nehemiah 4:5; Psalm 69:27-8; 109:6-15; Isaiah 2:9; Jeremiah 18:23.

Source: *The Times*, 28 January 1995.

147. Forgiveness

(Children, Concentration camps, Courage, Evil, Faith, Holocaust, Judgement, Love, Mercy, Murder, Nazism, Prayer, Second World War, Suffering)

This prayer was found on a scrap of paper beside the body of a child at Ravensbrück concentration camp:

O Lord, remember not only the men and women of
    goodwill,
but those of ill will.
But do not remember all the suffering they have inflicted
    upon us;
remember the fruits we have brought thanks to this
    suffering -
our comradeship, our loyalty, our humility, our courage,
    our generosity,
the greatness of heart which has grown out of all this;
and when they come to judgement,
let all the fruits which we have borne
be their forgiveness.

Bible references: Matthew 5:43-8; Luke 6:27-36; 23:34; Acts 7:60; Romans 12:14.

Source: Quoted in Russ Parker, *Free to Fail* (Triangle, 1992), pp 115-6.

148. Persecution

(Faith, Hymns, Presence of God, Singing, Suffering, Testimony)

Among the testimonies given at the World Charismatic Leaders' Conference in Brighton in 1991 was this remarkable story, shared by a Chinese pastor who spent eighteen years in prison for his faith.

'My friends wonder what kind of work I did in the labour camp to keep me physically healthy. I answered them that life in the labour camp was very, very hard. The authorities put me to emptying the human waste cesspool. But they did not know in those years how much I enjoyed working there.

'It was more than two metres in breadth and two metres in length, filled with human waste collected from the entire camp. Because the pit was so deep, I could not reach the bottom to empty it, so I had to walk into the disease-ridden mass, and scoop out successive layers of waste, all the time breathing the strong stench. The guards and all the prisoners kept a long way off because of the smell.

'So why did I enjoy working in the cesspool? In the labour camp all the prisoners were normally under strict surveillance, and no one could be alone. But when I worked in the cesspool I could be alone and could pray to our Lord as loudly as I needed. I could recite the Scriptures including all the Psalms I still remembered, and no one was close enough to

protest. That's the reason I enjoyed working in the cesspool.
Also I could sing loudly all the hymns I still remembered.

'When I worked in the cesspool I knew and discovered a
wonderful fellowship with our Lord. Again and again I sang
this hymn, and felt our Lord's presence with me:

> I come to the garden alone
> While the dew is still on the roses;
> And a voice I hear falling on my ear,
> The Son of God discloses.
> And he walks with me and he talks with me,
> And he tells me I am his own,
> And the joy we share as we tarry there
> None other has ever known.

'Again and again as I sang this hymn in the cesspool, I
experienced the Lord's presence. He never left me nor forsook
me. And so I survived, and the cesspool became my private
garden.'

Bible references: Matthew 5:11-12; Luke 6:22-3; Acts 5:41;
16:24-5; 2 Corinthians 1:3-11; 4:7-12; 6:4-10; 12:10;
Ephesians 5:19-20; Philippians 3:10-11; Colossians 1:24;
3:16-17; James 1:2-3; 1 Peter 1:6; 4:12-13, 16.

Source: Adapted from *Renewal*, October 1991.

149. Providence

*(Death, Faith, God, History, Plague, Pride, Protection,
Religion, Sickness, Suffering)*

During the Great Plague of 1665 it seemed at first as if

Christians were less prone to infection than the rest of the population, and some began to believe that their faith protected them from sickness, as the Protestant writer Richard Baxter noted. 'At first so few of the religiouser sort were taken away that (according to the mode of too many such) they began to be puffed up and boast of the great differences which God did make. But quickly after that they all fell alike.'

Bible references: Proverbs 16:18; Isaiah 28:15; Jeremiah 5:12-13; 14:13-16; 23:16-17; 27:9-15; Amos 9:10; Micah 3:11.

Source: Quoted in Herbert Butterfield, *Christianity and History* (Fontana, 1957), p 147.

150. Sin

(Evil, Human nature, Humility, Pride)

Many years ago, during an exchange of correspondence in *The Times* concerning the nature of evil, G. K. Chesterton wrote:

Dear Sirs,
You ask what is wrong with humanity. I am.
Yours sincerely,
G. K. Chesterton.

Bible references: Genesis 6:5; 8:21; 1 Kings 8:46; Job 15:14-16; Psalm 14:1-3; 143:2; Proverbs 20:9; Ecclesiastes 7:20; Jeremiah 17:9; Matthew 15:19; Mark 7:21-2; John 2:24-5; Romans 3:9, 23; Galatians 5:19-21.

Source: *Idea.*

151. Suffering

(Crucifixion, Incarnation, Pain, Presence of God, Sickness, Testimony)

Margaret Spufford was discovered to be suffering from acute osteoporosis at an unusually early age. She was coming home from one of her trips to hospital when the ambulancemen who were carrying her into the house tripped and stumbled.

> They dropped and then caught me. I can only have fallen a couple of inches, but the effect was terrifying. All my reflexes seemed to go berserk in the pain. I, who so much valued control, was completely out of control. I was screaming, not even able to stop in case my son could hear. My fingers were clenched in someone's hair, the world ran amok, and my husband, who was there, was utterly irrelevant through the pain. He could not reach me. Nor could anyone. 'She probably collapsed another vertebra or two,' said the hospital on the telephone, apparently. 'Just keep her quiet.'
>
> It was months before I dared tell even my husband, who was not likely to feel that I had suddenly been afflicted with religious mania, and knew I did not go in for pious or saccharine imagery, that quite extraordinarily at that moment of unreachability, I had suddenly been aware even as I screamed, of the presence of the Crucified. He did not cancel the moment, or assuage it, but was inside it.

Bible references: 2 Corinthians 1:3-11; 4:7-12; Philippians 3:10-11; 1 Peter 4:12-13.

Source: Margaret Spufford, *Celebration* (Fount, 1989), p 38.

152. Suffering

(Bible, Faith, God, Healing, Miracles, Pain, Sickness, Testimony)

Colin Dye is the pastor of Kensington Temple, one of London's largest churches, and widely respected as a preacher and teacher. He bears remarkable testimony to the way in which personal tragedy and suffering can actually serve to strengthen our faith, as he explains here.

Holding on to the promises and the goodness of God during times of suffering is the greatest challenge to faith. Yet this is the very thing that brings our faith to maturity and closer to its object, Jesus Christ. I have found this out in times of intense personal pain.

Our second daughter, Laura, suffered severe brain damage after birth due to an infection. The devastation and hurt this caused my wife and me are hard to describe. Despite the many improvements that we have seen that are nothing short of miracles in Laura's life, she is still totally dependent and virtually unable to do anything for herself. Our faith is passing through the fiery furnace, but we know God is the divine forger and he is working his purpose through it all.

Outside the Word of God, this is perhaps the single greatest cause of the growth of faith in my life.

Bible references: Job 23:10; Psalm 66:10; Proverbs 17:3; Isaiah 48:10; Zechariah 13:9; Malachi 3:3; James 1:2-3; 1 Peter 1:6-7; 4:12.

Source: *Renewal*, January 1996.

153. War

(Brothers, Families, Inequality, Politics, Poverty, Suffering, Wealth)

The civil war in Bosnia-Herzegovina divided not only communities but also families. As the Bosnian Serbs defended the town of Dornji Vakuf against the attacks of the Muslim government army, Serdjan and his brother Dadi were fighting for the government forces, while their other two brothers found themselves on the Serbian side. This terrible situation came about because the men's father was a Serb, and their mother a Muslim.

Serdjan and Dadi discovered what was happening when their sister Jasminka crossed from Serb-held territory and met her brothers in nearby Bugojno. There she told them that their brothers had been conscripted into the Serbian army. Serdjan said, 'There is a rule in every army: if you don't kill your enemy, he will kill you. Yet of course my brothers are not my enemies. I hope that somehow they can escape all this.' Serdjan knew he would not be involved in the final assault on the town: his foot was no more than a stump. But his brother Dadi would be there. 'I don't give a damn about politics,' he said. 'You never see the sons of the rich fighting on opposite sides, only the children of the poor.'

Bible references: Isaiah 19:2; Ezekiel 38:21.

Source: Adapted from *The Times*, 17 November 1994.

DEATH AND THE HEREAFTER

154. Awkwardness

(Afterlife, Foot in mouth, Heaven, Husbands, Platitudes, Wives, Humour)

A man bumped into an old friend he hadn't seen for ages. Naturally, his first question was how his friend was, and he received the standard English reply, 'Oh fine, thanks.' 'And how's your wife?' 'Oh, she's gone to be with the Lord' was the unexpected answer. 'Oh, I am sorry,' he said. That didn't sound quite right, so he tried again, 'Oh, I am glad.' No, come to think of it, that sounded even worse than his first response. So he had a third go: 'Oh, I am surprised.' At that point he changed the subject.

Source: Adapted from David Watson, Cambridge, February 1979.

155. Burial

(Afterlife, Eternity, Sleep, Humour)

Frenchman Henri Bidard achieved notoriety in 1963 when it was revealed that he spent each night sleeping in a coffin in his garden! The businessman said at his home in Argentan, 'After we die, most of us are destined to spend the rest of eternity inside a coffin. I wanted to get accustomed to being inside one *before* I die.'

Bible references: Job 7:7-10; 14:1-2; Psalm 39:4; 89:47-8; 90:5-6; 144:3-4; Isaiah 40:6-7; 1 Peter 1:24.

Source: Adapted from *Tombstone Humour* (Chancellor Press, 1993), p 372.

156. Disillusionment

(Children, Despair, Modern life, Parents, Politics, Terrorism, Violence)

Gudrun Ensslin was the girlfriend of Andreas Baader, the leader of the Red Army Faction, or 'Baader-Meinhof Gang' which terrorised West Germany in the 1970s. The path which took her there is a study in idealism, disillusionment and despair.

Her father was a pastor in the German Evangelical church, deeply committed to the struggle for social justice, disarmament and world peace. Gudrun grew up to share the views espoused by her parents. She attended Protestant youth gatherings and joined in the Lutheran hymns and songs for peace with equal fervour. She worked hard at school and studied in the Bible class at her father's church. She was going to be a teacher. She wanted to make the world a better place to live in.

When she left home and went to university she became more politically active. She campaigned hard for the Social Democratic Party in the election campaign of 1965. But when in the following year the party formed a Grand Coalition with the right-wing Christian Democrats, Ensslin felt betrayed. So she abandoned the mainstream SPD for the more extreme Socialist Student League. With them she demonstrated against the Vietnam war, pelted America House with eggs, distributed inflammatory leaflets, and wrecked the offices of university professors.

But soon that was not enough for her. Just as she had concluded that her father's Christianity wouldn't change the world, and then that politics couldn't, so now she decided that demonstrations wouldn't achieve anything either. The Nobel prize-winning novelist Günther Grass, who knew her in those days, said, 'She was idealistic, with an inborn loathing of any compromise. She had a yearning for the Absolute.' And so she teamed up with Andreas Baader and turned to 'direct action'. Together they set fire to shops, robbed banks and planted murderous bombs.

She was eventually arrested and sentenced to life imprisonment. In Stammheim prison she, like Baader and Meinhof, committed suicide.

Bible references: Ecclesiastes 2:20; 4:1-3; Proverbs 14:12; Matthew 27:3-5; Romans 6:23; 8:6; 2 Corinthians 7:10.

Source: Adapted from Jillian Becker, *Hitler's Children* (Granada, 1978).

157. Eternity

(Heaven, Local government, Peace, Remembrance, Second World War, War, Humour)

The small town of Morrinsville, near Auckland in New Zealand, decided to mark the fiftieth anniversary of VJ Day by creating its own monument with an eternal flame. Unfortunately the town council had not reckoned with the cost of the eternal gas supply. After receiving their first gas bill, councillors realised that they were facing running costs of about £8,500 per year, and decided that in this case eternity could not last for ever.

Bible references: Psalm 90:4; 2 Peter 3:8.

Source: Adapted from the *Daily Telegraph*, 31 August 1995.

158. Grief

(Afterlife, Burial, Children, Daughters, Faith, Families, Fathers, Heaven, Mourning, Parents, Prayer)

On 20 September 1542, Martin Luther's daughter Magdalena died aged just thirteen. His close companions recorded the great reformer's conversations at the time, and reveal the depth of Luther's grief, along with the strength of his faith. They also reveal how death was so much more a part of life in those days.

As his daughter was taking her last breaths he fell on his knees before her bed and prayed with bitter tears that God would spare her. Then she breathed her last in her father's arms. And he kept repeating, 'I so wanted to keep my darling daughter, for I love her dearly, if only our Lord God would leave her with me, but your will be done! Truly, nothing better, nothing better could have happened to her.' And after she had died he said, 'I am joyful in my spirit, but in the flesh I am so very sad. Parting pains one beyond measure. It is amazing: to know that she is certainly at peace, that all really is well, very well with her there, and yet to grieve so very much!'

And as she was laid in her coffin, he said, 'Dear little Leni! All has gone so well for you!' Then he burst into tears, and sighs shook his whole body, and he quickly went away. Then when he saw her lying in the coffin, he said, 'Oh you dear child, you must rise again and shine like the stars, yes, like the sun!' And as they hammered the nails in, he said: 'Hammer away! On the last day she will rise again!'

And as people came to accompany the coffin to the graveyard, and friends spoke to him and offered their sympathy, as was the custom, he answered: 'I have sent a saint to heaven, yes a living saint. O that we should die such a death! I would gladly accept such a death this very hour.'

Bible references: Matthew 5:4; 26:38-42; Mark 14:34-8; Luke 22:42; John 5:28-9; Romans 6:4-8; 8:11; Acts 21:13-14; 1 Corinthians 6:14; 15:22-3; 1 Thessalonians 4:13-17.

Source: Translated from R. Buchwald (ed.) *Luther im Gespräch* (Insel Verlag, 1983), pp 345-7.

159. Heaven

(Afterlife, Children, Faith, Families, Forgiveness, Grief, Love, Mourning, Murder, Peace, Prayer, Reconciliation, Repentance, Sin, Terrorism, Violence)

Bernadette Power lives in West Belfast with her three young children. Her husband Michael was killed as they drove to church one Sunday morning when a gunman opened fire on their car. He died in Bernadette's arms as the ambulance drove them to hospital; her oldest child, Michelle, was almost blinded by flying glass. Yet Bernadette radiates the love and peace of Christ, and shares her faith at every opportunity.

One morning the children were getting ready to go to school when her son Gavin asked, 'Mummy, will the man who killed Daddy be in heaven?' Bernadette offered up a quick prayer for help and answered, 'If those men are really sorry and ask Jesus to forgive them, then they will be in heaven.'

'Then I don't want to be in heaven, if they are there,' said Gavin.

What do you say to that? Bernadette gave the best answer she could. 'But if they really are sorry and admit that what they have done is a terrible sin and ask Jesus to forgive them, then God will change them. They will be different people in heaven.'

'Then let's pray that Jesus will heal them,' said Gavin.

Bible references: Psalm 51; Matthew 5:43-5; Luke 6:27-36; 23:34, 40-3; Acts 7:60, 26:20; Romans 12:17-21; 2 Corinthians 5:17; 7:10; 2 Peter 3:9; 1 John 1:9.

Source: Adapted from Cecil Kerr, in *Renewal*, May 1994.

160. Heaven

(Afterlife, Pride, Humour)

A Yorkshireman reached the pearly gates, and gave one of those sniffs they use in Yorkshire as a form of social comment. 'From Yorkshire, eh?' said the recording angel, wearily unlocking the gates. 'Well, you can come in, but I'm telling you now, you won't like it.'

Source: Adapted from John Sandilands, quoted in Margaret Pepper (ed.) *Dictionary of Religious Quotations* (Andre Deutsch, 1989), p 231.

161. Heaven

(Afterlife, Discipleship, Eternity, Faithfulness, Reward, Service, Treasure, Wealth, Witness)

St Peter was leading a new arrival around heaven. Back in her earthly life she had been very well-to-do, with a large and beautiful house and extensive garden, and she was hoping for something still finer in heaven. Indeed, Peter seemed to be leading her towards a huge and very attractive mansion which she hoped might be hers. He stopped outside and her hopes mounted.

'That's Joe's house,' he said, to her surprise. 'I believe you knew him.' She racked her brains for a moment, temporarily nonplussed. 'Joe?' she echoed. 'Not Joe the postman?' She had known him by sight from church and from her doorstep, but she couldn't imagine how he came to have such a splendid reward up here.

As if reading her thoughts, Peter explained. 'You see, during his time on earth Joe sent us up all sorts of materials to build with. The plot of land came from his Christian faith, but then he provided all the stone and timber for the house by his care and concern for others, and the furnishings by the way he shared his faith to enable other people to come here too.' 'Oh, I see,' the lady responded lamely, just beginning to see what that might mean for her.

Sure enough, as they went on their way the houses got progressively smaller and meaner, until eventually they turned into a narrow little side street and stopped in front of a tiny, shabby cottage. 'This is yours,' said Peter. 'I'm afraid it was the best we could manage with what you sent us.'

Bible references: Matthew 6:19-21; 16:27; 19:21; Mark 10:21; Luke 12:33-4; 16:9; 18:22; 1 Corinthians 3:9-15; 4:5; 2 Corinthians 5:10; Ephesians 2:20-2; 1 Timothy 6:17-19; Revelation 22:12.

Source: Adapted from Roy Etherton, Sevenoaks 1982.

162. Last words

(Afterlife, Alcohol, Bible, God, Heaven, Hell, Judgement, Life, Humour)

People's last recorded words can be ironic, amusing or defiant, as the following examples show:
- 'They couldn't hit an elephant at this dist…': General Sedgewick (d. 1864) as he looked over the parapet at the enemy in the American Civil War.
- 'Dear me, I must be turning into a god': Emperor

Vespasian (AD79).

- 'I've had eighteen straight whiskies. I think that's the record.... After thirty-nine years, this is all I've done': Dylan Thomas, poet (d. 1953).
- 'I want to go to hell, not to heaven, for there I shall enjoy the company of popes, kings and princes, while in heaven are only beggars, monks and apostles': Niccolo Machiavelli, political theorist (d. 1530).
- 'In the name of God, let me die in peace!': Voltaire, atheist philosopher (d. 1778) to a priest by his bedside, hoping for a last-minute conversion. Then, as the bedside lamp flared up, 'The flames already?'
- 'Either this wallpaper goes, or I do': Oscar Wilde, dramatist and wit (d. 1900).
- 'Begone, you and your trumpery! Until this moment I believed that there was neither a God nor a hell. Now I know and feel that there are both and that I am doomed to perdition by the just judgement of the Almighty': Thomas Scott, lawyer and U.S. Congressman (d. 1887), to the priest at his deathbed.
- 'Lord, open the King of England's eyes!': William Tyndale, Bible translator, strangled at the stake in 1536.

Bible references: Matthew 10:28; Luke 6:20-6; 16:19-31; 12:4-5; Acts 26:18; 2 Corinthians 4:4.

Source: Quoted in Jonathon Green, *Famous Last Words* (Chancellor Press, 1993).

163. Martyrdom

(Faith, Murder, Persecution, Suffering, Testimony, Torture, Witness)

In February 1994, Bishop Haik Hovsepian-Mehr, leader of the Assemblies of God in Iran, was abducted and murdered. It was surely no coincidence that this happened shortly after he had secured the release of a fellow Christian named Mehdi Dibaj, who had been threatened with execution for apostasy (that is, converting to Christianity). Bishop Haik's name had already become familiar in the West through his appeal to the United Nations in 1993 to investigate the abuse of human rights against evangelical Christians in Iran, including the closure of churches, imprisonment without charge, torture and execution. The day before he vanished, never to be seen alive again, the bishop wrote a 'Letter to Friends'.

Praise the Lord for all his victories! Brother Dibaj has just arrived in our house. When he entered the house all believers started to sing, 'In the name of Jesus, we have the victory.' This was the best salutation they could offer to our hero. All Christians are happy and are congratulating one another. They have got the feeling that perhaps no other Muslim convert will be executed merely for his beliefs in Iran. They feel that this will bring many people to Christ.

But we should keep in mind the persecutions that other converts are going through. If those enemies of the cross continue their new strategy of persecution, we may lose all our converts. I know it is playing with fire, but I am ready to die for the cause of the church so that others will be able to worship their Lord peacefully and without so much fear. Please pray with us that the Lord will solve all other problems.

The columnist Bernard Levin, himself not a Christian, commented, 'We can safely say that he was tortured and murdered because he was a Christian and for the support he was always ready to give to his brother and sister Christians. Such a man, though he be dead, cannot be forgotten.'

Bible references: Acts 4:23-31; 5:41; 9:16; 20:17-38; 21:10-14; Romans 14:7-8; Philippians 1:20-4; 2 Timothy 2:8-13.

Source: *The Times*, 15 February 1994.

164. Obituary

(Heaven, Hell, Journalism, Judgement, Media, Newspapers, Humour)

A London newspaper once mistakenly printed the obituary of a well-known politician while he was still alive. During the course of the morning the editor received an outraged phone call from the man in question. 'I've just read my obituary in your paper!' he spluttered. 'I see,' replied the quick-thinking editor, 'And may I ask where you are speaking from?'

Source: Adapted from Alister McGrath, *Understanding the Trinity* (Kingsway, 1987), p 11.

165. Resurrection

(Burial, Heaven, Practical joke, Sleep, Humour)

A Texan was once the victim of a practical joke. His friends put a sedative in his drink in the evening, then when he was sound asleep, buried him in an open coffin in an open grave in the cemetery. Next morning he woke up among the tombs, not knowing where he was or what had happened. As he looked around and gradually realised where he was lying, he burst out excitedly, 'Hallelujah! It's resurrection day and a Texan is the first to be raised!'

Source: Adapted from Billy Graham, Cambridge, 17 February 1980.

166. Suicide

(Bitterness, Despair, Drugs, Families, Modern life, Parents, Young people)

He wasn't well known. We don't even know his name. But his farewell note was printed in a local newspaper, then a national magazine. It read: 'Now I am going to end it all, because all a junkie gives to his friends and relatives is trouble, worry, bitterness and despair. It's not just himself he destroys, but other people too. Thanks to my dear parents and my little gran. Physically I'm nothing. Being a junkie is always the pits. Let this be a warning to anyone who's ever thinking about the decision: Will I try it? You cretins, look at me. No more worries, now, Simone – good luck.'

Bible references: Job 15:20-35; Proverbs 14:12; Romans 6:23; 8:6; 2 Corinthians 7:10; Galatians 6:7-8; James 1:15.

Source: Translated from 'Wir Kinder vom Bahnhof Zoo', *Stern* magazine.

FAMILY LIFE

167. Anniversaries

(Husbands, Marriage, Records, Renewal of vows, Weddings, Wives)

You sometimes hear of a couple who renew their marriage vows, usually to mark some special occasion, such as their twenty-fifth wedding anniversary. But Jack and Edna Moran of Seattle so enjoyed getting married the first time round that they kept on getting married over and over again. The first time was in 1937 in the United States, but they then repeated it on no fewer than forty occasions, in locations as diverse as Cairo, Canada and Westminster Abbey in London.

If that's the record for the world's most married couple, the longest recorded marriage lasted for eighty-six years. It was between Sir Temulji Bhiaji Nariman and Lady Nariman, but they did have a head-start over most couples in that they got married at the age of only five!

Bible references: Genesis 2:20-4; Matthew 19:4-6; Mark 10:6-9; Ephesians 5:25-31; Colossians 3:19.

173

Source: Adapted from Simon Mayo and Martin Wroe, *The Big Match* (Marshall Pickering, 1993), p 89.

168. Bigamy

(Families, Husbands, Marriage, Records, Wives)

The world record for bigamous marriages is 104, by a man named Fred Jipp between 1949 and 1981. He had wives in fifteen different countries and twenty-eight states of America. When the deception was discovered, he was sentenced to six years in prison for bigamy (about twenty days per wife) and twenty-eight years for fraud: an interesting sense of priorities!

Bible references: 1 Timothy 3:2, 12; Titus 1:6.

Source: Adapted from Simon Mayo and Martin Wroe, *The Big Match* (Marshall Pickering, 1993), p 93.

169. Divorce

(Children, Daughters, Families, Father, Marriage, Pain, Promises)

The following piece was written by fourteen-year-old Vicki Kraushaar in the American Girl Scouts' magazine, *American Girl*.

When I was ten, my parents got a divorce. Naturally, my

father told me about it, because he was my favourite.

'Honey, I know it's been kind of bad for you these past few days, and I don't want to make it worse. But there's something I have to tell you. Honey, your mother and I got a divorce.'

'But, Daddy – '

'I know you don't want this, but it has to be done. Your mother and I just don't get along like we used to. I'm already packed, and my plane is leaving in half an hour.'

'But, Daddy, why do you have to leave?'

'Well honey, your mother and I can't live together any more.'

'I know that, but I mean why do you have to leave town?'

'Oh. Well, I got someone waiting for me in New Jersey.'

'But, Daddy, will I ever see you again?'

'Sure you will, honey. We'll work something out.'

'But what? I mean, you'll be living in New Jersey, and I'll be living here in Washington.'

'Maybe your mother will agree to you spending two weeks in the summer and two in the winter with me.'

'Why not more often?'

'I don't think she'll agree to two weeks in the summer and two in the winter, much less more.'

'Well, it can't hurt to try.'

'I know, honey, but we'll have to work it out later. My plane leaves in twenty minutes and I've got to get to the airport. Now I'm going to get my luggage, and I want you to go to your room so you don't have to watch me. And no long goodbyes either.'

'Okay Daddy. Goodbye. Don't forget to write.'

'I won't. Goodbye. Now go to your room.'

'Okay. Daddy, I don't want you to go.'

'I know, honey. But I have to.'

'Why?'

'You wouldn't understand, honey.'

'Yes, I would.'

'No, you wouldn't.'

'Oh well. Goodbye.'

'Goodbye. Now go to your room. Hurry up.'

'Okay. Well, I guess that's the way life goes sometimes.'

'Yes, honey. That's the way life goes sometimes.'

After my father walked out that door, I never heard from him again.

Bible references: Malachi 2:13-16; Matthew 5:31-2; 19:3-9; Mark 10:2-12; Luke 16:18; Romans 7:2-3; 1 Corinthians 7:10-11.

Source: Quoted in James C. Dobson, *Straight Talk* (Hodder and Stoughton, 1993), pp 76-8.

170. Divorce

(Alpha, Conversion, Families, Holy Spirit, Hope, Love, Marriage, Reconciliation)

Michael and Sharon Lovatt had been married for nine years, and had five children aged between fifteen months and nine. But their marriage was going nowhere, they were growing apart, and Michael was drinking too much. One Christmas Day he popped out for an hour at lunchtime and didn't come back until four o'clock, by which time the children had opened all their presents and were desperate for their Christmas dinner. By the following September it all seemed hopeless, and they decided they would go their separate ways. Then early in the new year Sharon's mother told them about a wonderful course called Alpha, and they agreed to go on it together. Sharon soon made a commitment to Christ, but Michael seemed more sceptical.

On 24th February they went off for an Alpha away-day – shortly after the legal papers had come through granting them a degree nisi. That afternoon Michael gave his life to Jesus. And suddenly, quite dramatically, everything changed. They found that the love which they thought had died reawakened. A few weeks after their decree absolute came through, Michael proposed to Sharon, and she accepted. They were remarried on Sharon's thirtieth birthday. She says, 'We have still got an awful lot of things that we are trying to work through. But with the Lord's help we will get there eventually. Relationships are being mended. For the first time in my life I feel really loved. We are a real family now. Our lives have been changed for good. It's wonderful.'

Bible references: 1 Corinthians 7:13-16; 2 Corinthians 5:17-20; 1 Peter 3:1-2.

Source: *SEE* (Southwell Diocesan newspaper), quoted in *Alpha News*, July 1996.

171. Divorce

(Children, Families, Inequality, Marriage, Modern life, Parenthood)

According to a long-term study, children whose parents divorce while they are young not only suffer trauma at the time, but also experience ill-effects into adult life. They tend to leave school with fewer qualifications and are more likely to be unemployed. They are more likely to leave home early, marry in their teens and have children before the age of twenty-three. They are more prone to emotional or psychological problems, especially if they are women. By their early forties they are more likely to have lost touch with their parents, even the one who brought them up.

Professor A.H. Halsey of Oxford University, who is the Professor of Social and Administrative Studies, put it trenchantly: 'On the evidence available, such children tend to die earlier, to have more illness, to do less well at school, to exist at a lower level of nutrition, comfort and conviviality, to suffer more unemployment, to be more prone to deviance and crime, and finally to repeat the cycle of unstable parenting from which they themselves have suffered.'

Bible references: Jeremiah 31:29; Ezekiel 18:2; Malachi 2:13-16; Matthew 5:31-2; 19:3-9; Mark 10:2-12; Luke 16:18; Romans 7:2-3; 1 Corinthians 7:10-11.

Source: National Survey of Health and Development and National Child Development Survey (1991) quoted in *LandMARC*, summer 1992; A.H. Halsey quoted by David Holloway in *New Directions*, September 1995.

172. Expectations

(Communication, Differences, Families, Holidays, Husbands, Lifestyle, Love, Marriage, Parents, Personality, Wives)

Shortly before their first wedding anniversary, Bill Hybels told his wife Lynne that he was planning a holiday. 'Oh great,' she replied, 'Where are we going?' 'No, you don't understand,' he said, 'I said *I* am going on vacation.' 'Not without me you're not!' was her immediate – and angry – rejoinder.

The problem was that Bill's parents had been used to taking separate holidays, as well as times away together. His father would ring his mother up from the airport and tell her he was off to South Africa for five weeks: in the Hybels household, this was normal behaviour for a husband and wife. But Lynne's parents had always done everything together; they hated spending even one night apart. For her, Bill's suggestion that he wanted to go away on his own without her showed that he didn't love her any more, and that their marriage was doomed.

Once they had talked all this through, and had each found out where the other was coming from, the problem could be resolved. But it just goes to show how different people are, and how contrasting expectations can act as unexploded bombs within relationships, ticking away until some innocent remark triggers them off.

Bible references: Romans 12:10, 16; 1 Corinthians 13:4-7; Ephesians 5:21-33; Colossians 3:18-19; James 1:19.

Source: Adapted from Bill and Lynne Hybels, *Fit to be Tied* (Zondervan, 1991), pp 93-4.

173. Father and son

(Alpha, Children, Conversion, Divorce, Drugs, Evangelism, Families, Forgiveness, Love, Parenthood, Reconciliation, Testimony)

Paul and Clinton Cowley didn't exactly have a very good

father and son relationship. Paul had been a bit of a lad in his time: as a skinhead he'd got a criminal record for stealing cars and joy-riding. But he found what he was looking for in the army. He worked hard and applied himself, and soon rose through the ranks. He got married and had a little boy, Clinton, but the combination of his ambition and a number of affairs with other women soon led to a divorce. Clinton went to live with his mother and only saw Paul once or twice a year.

But then something happened to change Paul's life. When his mother died, he found a Bible among her possessions, with lots of passages marked. He hadn't known his mother was interested in that sort of thing, but discovered that she'd become a Christian two years before. He decided to go to church, and after various false starts, he ended up at Holy Trinity Brompton, where he went on an Alpha course. He ended up committing himself to Christ, and as he puts it, got a whole new perspective on life. One of his new priorities was to be reconciled with Clinton, and he began praying regularly that they could get together and start again.

Meanwhile, Clinton had begun to get into trouble at secondary school; in his own words: 'burning stuff down, smashing stuff, fighting all the time, starting gang fights, bunking off school'. It wasn't long before he was dabbling in drugs – dope, speed, acid, and then dealing in order to fund his habit. One night everything seemed to come to a head. 'I just sat there and said to the sky, "If there is somebody out there, then you'd better help me now, because I am going to die soon from an overdose or something."' Next morning, his mother gave him his father's telephone number. He rang up and agreed to go to London to meet him. It was six years since they'd last seen each other. Paul says, 'I turned up at King's Cross and saw him walking towards me. I had left a little cute boy, but now this "thug" was walking towards me. He had dark glasses on and a small suitcase. It frightened the life out of me.'

Clinton stayed in London with Paul and his new wife, and eventually went on an Alpha course himself. As it had done with Paul, it changed Clinton's life. He says, 'I am 100 per cent Christian now. I still have my difficulties, like everybody does. I still have my temptations, but I am getting so much stronger. When I took drugs I lost everything. I lost my family, I lost my friends, I lost my home, every penny I had, my decency and my respect. God has totally transformed my life. I know God has forgiven me. I pray constantly. My relationship with my Dad is very very strong. We have worked through a lot of stuff. I have completely forgiven him.'

Bible references: Genesis 46:29; Malachi 4:6; Luke 1:17; 15:11-32; 2 Corinthians 5:17-20; Ephesians 2:1-5; 6:4; Colossians 3:21; Titus 3:3-7.

Source: Adapted from *Alpha News*, July 1996.

174. Marriage

(Eden, Fishing, Husbands, Wives, Humour)

In paradise, Adam went fishing one day. He didn't return that night, nor the next, and when he finally got back after a three-day absence, Eve greeted him very suspiciously.
'Where've you been all this time?' she demanded.
'Just fishing,' he answered.
'Where are all the fish, then?' she asked. 'And why were you gone so long?'
Adam lamely protested that the fish hadn't bitten, and that he'd enjoyed sitting by the lake, but Eve wasn't satisfied. 'Are

you sure you haven't been seeing someone else?' she enquired.

'But darling,' replied Adam, 'how could there be? You know you're the only woman in the world!'

All the same, that night, after Adam had gone to sleep, Eve lifted back the covers and carefully counted his ribs.

Bible references: Genesis 2:20-4.

Source: Adapted from Jonathan Perkin, Bath 1992.

175. Marriage

(Death,   Epitaphs,   Husbands,   Love,   Misunderstanding, Quarrels, Wives, Humour)

Tombstones often bear witness to the love of husband and wife, but occasionally they reveal that all was not as happy as might have been, as these examples show.

From Farmington cemetery in the United States:

ELIZA ANN
has gone to rest
She now reclines on Abraham's breast
Peace at last for Eliza Ann
But not for Father Abraham.

To show that it is not just women who were portrayed in this way, there is the tomb of Michael Collins in Gravesend, Kent:

Beneath this stone lies one whose life
Was spent in quarrels and in strife
Wake not his spirit from its rest
For when he slept the world was blest.

Occasionally the wording didn't come out quite as intended, as at Easingwold in Yorkshire:

She lived with her husband fifty years
And died in the confident hope of a better life.

Or at St Saviour's church in Hackney, East London:
Here lies the body of JAMES ROBINSON
and RUTH his wife.
'Lord, their warfare is accomplished'

Bible references: Proverbs 19:13; 20:3; 21:9, 19; 25:24; 26:21; 27:15; Isaiah 40:2; 1 Timothy 6:4.

Source: Quoted in *Tombstone Humour* (Chancellor Press, 1993), pp 64-5, 67, 81.

176. Parenthood

(Bedtime, Busyness, Children, Daughters, Families, Fathers, Stories, Time)

A father used to read a bedtime story to his four-year-old daughter, but every single night she asked for the same one: Goldilocks and the Three Bears. After the umpteenth time he'd read it he had a great idea which would keep them both happy. He recorded the story on tape. So when that night she again asked for her favourite story, he explained to her that all she needed to do was to press the button and she would hear him reading the story. That way he could save himself some time and she could hear the story. 'But Daddy,' she said, 'I can't sit on the tape recorder's lap!'

Bible references: Ephesians 6:4; Colossians 3:21.

Source: Adapted from Gordon and Gail Macdonald, *Till the Heart be Touched* (Highland Books, 1992), pp 23-4.

177. Parenthood

(Busyness, Children, Families, Listening, Mothers, Sons, Time)

A letter from a runaway son in the United States:

Dear Folks,
    Thank you for everything, but I am going to Chicago to try and start a new life. You asked me why I gave you so much trouble, and the answer is easy for me to give you, but I wonder if you will understand.

    Remember when I was about six or seven and I used to want you to just listen to me? I remember all the nice things you gave me for Christmas and my birthday, and I was really happy with the things – for about a week – but the rest of the time I didn't really want presents. I just wanted you to listen to me like I was somebody who felt things too. But you said you were busy.

Mum, you're a wonderful cook, and you have everything so clean and you were so tired so much from doing all those things that made you busy, but you know something, Mum? I would have liked crackers and peanut butter just as much, if you had only sat down with me during the day and said to me: 'Tell me all about it so I can maybe help you understand.'

I think that all the kids who are doing so many things that grownups are tearing out their hair worrying about are really looking for somebody that will have time to listen a few minutes and who really will treat them as they would a grownup who might be useful to them, you know – polite to them. If you folks had ever said to me, 'Pardon me' when you interrupted me, I'd have dropped dead.

If anybody asks you where I am, tell them I've gone looking for somebody with time, because I've got a lot of things I want to talk about.

Love to all,

Your son.

Bible references: Ephesians 6:4; Colossians 3:21; James 1:19.

Source: Quoted in Gordon Macdonald, *The Effective Father* (Highland Books, 1989), pp 85-6.

178. Pressure and pain

(Children, Church, Conversion, Crime, Drugs, Families, Freedom, Hope, Modern life, Parents, Salvation, Suffering)

Sometimes Christian parents fail to appreciate the pressures on their children in modern society, including the pressure to take drugs. Jeremy Parr of Yeldall Christian Centre and his stepson Leigh have courageously described how their relationship was torn apart by drug addiction.

'I got very angry with God,' said Leigh. 'Jeremy was a lay preacher and I saw them supporting other young people and I felt like the church was taking him away from me. We had done a lot, but he became very busy with work and church. Someone at college gave me cannabis. Then I got in with a crowd of people where I lived. I got accepted by a group of people who had given up. I didn't have to prove anything to these people.'

As Leigh's addiction got worse, Jeremy's business folded, and he and his wife left their church. 'The church didn't understand,' he said. 'They had no comprehension of what we were feeling. We felt that we were failures as parents because of what was happening and we were not supported or encouraged to think that we weren't. I have spoken to church leaders whose children have taken drugs who say to me, "We can't tell the church because of how we believe they will react."'

By the time Leigh was nineteen he was addicted to heroin, burgling shops to fund his habit, and worried that he was becoming paranoid and psychotic on the drugs. He was briefly imprisoned for attacking someone, and was overdosing, either by accident or because 'life had no real worth'. His relationship with his family had broken down completely. 'Youngsters dabbling today just don't realise what it does to you in the long term,' he said. 'Every addict who's

been an addict for a long time says, "I'm gonna give this up."
It's a real prison.'

For Leigh, the breakthrough came when he met an
evangelist named Steve Butcher. 'That's when I realised the
importance of knowing God. I had come to a point of total
desperation and I realised there was hope. For me, Jesus is the
answer. He's a solid rock who transcends all this crap of
thinking drugs are gonna make you happy.' He now has a job
on a farm in Devon and has been drug-free for a year. His
relationship with his parents has been restored, and he is clear
about what made the difference. 'I have only seen freedom
come through Christ. I really haven't seen it come through
anything else. They relapse. They need the hope that Christ
offers.'

Bible references: Isaiah 61:1; Malachi 4:6; Luke 1:17; 4:18;
15:11-32; John 8:31-6; Romans 6:16-23; 8:2, 15; 2
Corinthians 5:17-20; Galatians 4:3-7; Ephesians 2:1-5, 6:4;
Colossians 3:21; Titus 3:3-7.

Source: Adapted from the *Church of England Newspaper*, 17
May 1996.

179. Sex

*(Cats, Honeymoon, Marriage, Spinsters, Weddings, Women,
Humour)*

Two sisters lived together and had the reputation of being
virulently anti-men. They scared off all potential suitors, and
it was rare that a man even set foot inside the house. They
were so zealous that when they got a cat – female, of course –

they would never let her out at night, just in case there were any sex-crazed tomcats on the prowl.

But eventually the day came when one of the sisters was wooed and won, to her companion's dismay, and got married. A week after the wedding her sister was surprised to get a postcard from the honeymoon resort, and even more surprised by the message. It simply said, 'Let the cat out!'

Bible references: Genesis 2:20-4; Matthew 19:10-12; 1 Corinthians 7:7-9.

Source: Adapted from Jonathan Perkin, Bath 1992.

180. Wedding

(Bachelors, Brides, Marriage, Practical jokes, Sheep, Humour)

When two of his mates announced their engagements, Welshman John Bennett of Ystrad Deri decided that he didn't want to be left out. So he sent out engagement announcements, organised a stag night, and invited his friends and family to the ceremony at Tredegar Register Office, followed by a reception. The guests were somewhat surprised at the speed of events, as they had not previously heard John talk about Gerwyn, his bride-to-be.

When the day came and the guests assembled, they were even more surprised when they were introduced to Gerwyn. True, she was unmarried – and she was all in white – but she was a sheep! 'Luckily everyone saw the funny side,' commented the thirty-five-year-old 'groom.' 'We took some pictures of the bride, put her back in her field, and then went ahead with the reception anyway.'

Source: Adapted from the *South Wales Echo*, quoted in the *Daily Telegraph*, 27 August 1994.

MONEY, MONEY, MONEY

181. Beatitudes

(Bible, Economics, Life, Modern life, Poverty, Power, Reward, Wealth, Humour)

From the Gospel according to Mammon:
Blessed are the rich, for they inherited the earth some time ago, although the rest of you may buy shares in it so long as you can afford the broking charges.
Blessed are the powerful, but that goes without saying.
Blessed are those who hunger and thirst after money, for they shall be called enterprising.
Blessed are you when men envy and admire you, for then you will have become a member of the competitive economy.
And as for the poor, the meek, the old, the sick and the persecuted, you will get your reward in heaven.
This is the word of Mammon.

Bible references: Psalm 37:11; Matthew 5:3-10; 6:24; 19:23-6; Mark 10:23-7; Luke 6:20-6; 16:13; 18:24-7; 1 Timothy 6:9-10, 17.

Source: Martin Wroe, Nick McIvor and Simon Parke, *The '101' Survivors' Guide to the Church* (Monarch, 1990), p 58.

182. Bequests

(Fellowship,   Giving,   Neighbours,   Prayer,   Pubs, Reconciliation, Wills, Humour)

In his will of May 1491, Robert Halliday of Eastcheap, London, bequeathed the sum of five pounds per annum to the churchwardens for the following purpose:

> Either to make an entertainment among such persons of his home parish of St Clement, who should be at variance with each other, in the week preceding Easter, to induce such persons to be better neighbours and to beget brotherly love amongst them; or if none should be found in the said parish, then to make an entertainment with the said money at the tavern among the honest parishioners of the said parish on the day common called Shere Thursday, that they may pray more fervently.

Bible references: Psalm 133:1; Luke 16:9; Romans 12:10; 12:13; 1 Thessalonians 4:9-10; Hebrews 13:1; 1 Peter 1:22; 2 Peter 1:5-8.

Source: Quoted in *Tombstone Humour* (Chancellor Press, 1993), pp 138-9.

183. Capitalism

(Contentment, Economics, Fishing, Wealth)

One fine day, a capitalist was walking along the quayside when he saw a fisherman stretched out idly beside his boat, placidly smoking his pipe. 'Why aren't you out in your boat catching fish?' asked the capitalist. 'Because I've already been out once today, and caught all the fish I needed,' was the laconic reply.

'But why don't you go out again and catch some more?' insisted the capitalist.

'And why would I want to do that?' the fisherman asked, bemused.

'So that you can make more money,' was the confident reply. 'Then you could buy yourself a bigger and better boat, with better fishing tackle too.'

'But what would I do then?' asked the fisherman, clearly unconvinced.

'Why, then you could catch even more fish, and make even more money.'

'Yes, but *then* what would I do?' persisted the fisherman.

'Well,' said the capitalist, 'then you could sit back and enjoy life.'

'Can't you see?' retorted the fisherman. 'That's exactly what I'm doing now!'

Bible references: Ecclesiastes 2:24-6; 3:12-13, 22; 5:10-12, 18-19; 9:7; Proverbs 30:8-9; Philippians 4:11-12; 1 Timothy 6:6-10; Hebrews 13:5.

Source: Adapted from Michael Marshall, the *Church of England Newspaper*, 31 March 1995.

184. Church treasurers

(Giving, Humour)

A strong man with a stall at a travelling fair included in his act a challenge to the spectators. As they watched, he squeezed the juice out of an orange with his bare hands, then offered five pounds to anyone who could get another drop of juice out of the fruit. Several strapping young men jumped onto the stage and tried their luck, but even though they strained with all their might, they couldn't get a drop out. Then a weedy-looking fellow climbed up onto the stage and took the orange in his hand. He examined the fruit, then squeezed it carefully, and to the crowd's amazement and delight, out came not just one, but two drops of juice. As the strong man handed over the money, he said, 'You're the first person that's ever managed to get any juice out. If you don't mind me asking, how did you do it?' 'It wasn't difficult,' replied the man. 'You see, I'm a church treasurer. I regularly have to get blood out of a stone.'

Bible references: Malachi 3:8-10.

Source: unknown.

185. Collection

(Bible, Church, Generosity, Giving, Offertory, Prayer, Silence, Humour)

'The pastor's inflection suggested he was coming towards the end and the offering was next. Clarence eased his wallet out and saw he had no cash. He got out a pen and hid the cheque-book in his Bible (next to Psalm 101) and quietly scratched out a cheque for thirty dollars, more than usual, because his offering was personalized. He wrote surreptitiously, trying to keep his eyes up and ahead – knowing you're not supposed to write cheques in church, it isn't a grocery store.

'He glanced to his right, and Mrs Val Tollefson was glaring at him. She thought he was writing in his Bible. (In the old Norwegian synod you didn't write in a Bible, not even little comments in the margin like "Good verse" or "You can say that again", because every word in the Bible is true and you shouldn't add any that might not be true, not even in pencil, because it undermines the authority of Scripture.) Meanwhile, the sermon ended and Pastor Ingqvist launched into prayer. Clarence tried to tear the cheque quietly out of the chequebook. There's no worse sound in the sanctuary than a cheque ripping. His cheque wouldn't come quietly, the first half-inch rip sounded like plywood being torn from a wall, so he waited for the pastor to launch into a strong sentence of fervent prayer to cover up the cheque removal, but Pastor Ingqvist was pausing at odd points, so Clarence couldn't tell when it was safe or when suddenly he would be ripping in the middle of pure holy silence. Clarence folded the cheque back and forth until it almost fell off. Mrs. Tollefson was about to get up and snatch Scripture out of his hands. At prayers' end, as they said the Lord's Prayer, he eased the cheque out, and when Elmer passed the basket, Clarence laid down the cheque folded neatly in half in the basket and bowed his head and suddenly realised he had written it for three hundred dollars.

'He had written with his eyes averted and he knew he had written three-zero-zero on the short line and three-zero-zero on the long line. Could a man sneak downstairs after church and find the deacons counting the collection and say, "Fellows, there's been a mistake. I gave more than I really wanted to"?'

Bible references: Mark 12:41-4; Luke 21:1-4; 1 Corinthians 16:1-2; 2 Corinthians 8:12; 9:6-15.

Source: Garrison Keillor, *Leaving Home* (Faber and Faber, 1987), pp 82-3.

186. Giving

(Collection, Commandments, Commitment, Discipleship, Generosity, Offertory, Preaching, Saints)

An elderly retired civil servant in Ireland was at Mass one morning when the Gospel reading was the story of the rich young man. He heard the words of Jesus as a command addressed directly to him: 'Sell everything you have and give to the poor, and you will have treasure in heaven. Then come, follow me.' So he put all the money he had in his pockets in the poor box on his way out of church, and set off to walk the 135 miles to the pilgrimage centre at Lough Derg. When he failed to come home, his family were concerned and contacted the police, who eventually tracked him down. He was examined by a doctor and placed in a mental hospital: his wife believed he was suffering from an illness called 'religious mania'. Although the man himself fully understood what was happening to him, he accepted it as God's will, and it was only with some difficulty that the hospital persuaded his wife to agree to his discharge.

The Irish psychiatrist M. O'Connor Drury noted wryly that St Anthony the Hermit had heard exactly the same words read out in a church in Alexandria some 1,600 years earlier, and had responded in precisely the same way, by walking out into the desert to found the Christian eremitical tradition. He was not certified, but canonised.

Bible references: Matthew 6:19-21; 19:21; Mark 10:21; 12:41-4; Luke 12:33-4; 16:9; 18:22; 21:1-4; Acts 2:45; 4:34-5; 1 Timothy 6:19.

Source: Adapted from M. O'Connor Drury, *The Danger of Words*, quoted in David Hay, *Exploring Inner Space* (Mowbray, 1987), pp 172-3.

187. Lottery

(Death, Despair, Gambling, Suicide, Wealth)

In April 1995, the *Daily Mail* reported the sad story of a fifty-one-year-old man who committed suicide as a direct result of the national lottery.

He regularly bought a batch of tickets and always used the same numbers. On checking his tickets one week, he discovered that he had all the winning numbers, meaning a win for his family and a friend of one million pounds each! However, on checking the dates on the tickets he realised to his horror that they had expired the previous week, and were therefore absolutely worthless. In a state of shock he went upstairs and shot himself.

A police spokesperson said, 'The man had obviously flipped. He was a church-goer and a very fine man with no dark side to his character. You can never judge what people are capable of at times of stress.'

A neighbour added, 'He was the nicest man in our street. He worked for the church and was always visiting the sick.'

The tragedy came as less of a surprise to the local newsagent, from whom the man had bought the lottery tickets. He commented, 'The national lottery does strange things to people. They become obsessed. For some of my customers it is all they seem to live for. They spend their last pennies on it each week. It is very sad that these are the extremes gambling can lead to.'

Bible references: Matthew 6:24; 13:22; 16:26; Mark 4:18-19; 8:36; Luke 8:14; 12:15; 16:13; 1 Timothy 6:9-10.

Source: Quoted by Keith Tondeur in *Renewal*, August 1995.

188. Lottery

(Friendship, Gambling, Happiness, Human nature, Wealth)

Everybody knows that money doesn't buy you happiness, yet still millions of people buy lottery tickets each week in the hope that they will win millions. The sad fact is that some of the 'lucky' winners turn out to be not so lucky after all.

Fred Baker, aged sixty-four, was one of a syndicate of elderly people who shared one of the very first lottery jackpots. But after the group of friends won over £200,000 each, they stopped getting together. Mr Baker said, 'We used to meet two or three times a week, but that has stopped now. Since I won the money, I have been more lonely than ever before.'

Bible references: Proverbs 30:8-9; Matthew 13:22; 16:26; Mark 8:36; 1 Timothy 6:9-10, 17; Revelation 3:17.

Source: Adapted from the *Daily Telegraph*, 13 May 1995.

189. Meanness

(Church, Collection, Giving, Offertory, Humour)

The old miser put five pence in the offertory bag at church, and at the end of the service watched the treasurer taking the bags away. 'Where does that money go, young man?' he asked. 'It is for the Lord,' came the answer. 'Well I'll be seeing him long before you do,' replied the old man, 'so I think I'll take it to him myself.'

Bible references: Proverbs 11:24; 28:22; Malachi 3:8-10; Matthew 6:22-3; Luke 11:34-6; Acts 5:1-10; 2 Corinthians 9:6-7.

Source: unknown.

190. Tithing

(Commitment, Discipleship, Generosity, Giving, Wealth)

The name Laing is familiar from countless construction sites across the United Kingdom. The former company president Sir John Laing, who died in 1978, was throughout his life a careful and generous steward of the resources God gave to him. At the age of thirty his building business was in severe financial difficulty. But he made a commitment which he later summed up in these words: 'First, the centre of my life was to be God – God as seen in Jesus Christ. Secondly, I was going to enjoy life and help others to enjoy it.' To this end, in 1909 he drew up a financial plan to determine his present and future giving: 'If income is £2,000 per year, give £200, live on £500, save £1,300. If income is £4,000 per year, give £1,500, live on £500, save £2,000.' When Sir John's will was published after his death, many people were amazed at the size of his estate: just £371. As his biographer commented, 'The man who had handled millions had given them all away.'

Bible references: 1 Chronicles 29:2-17; Job 31:24-8; Proverbs 3:9-10; 10:4; 11:24-5; 22:9; Malachi 3:10; Mark 4:24-5; Luke 6:38; Acts 11:29-30; 20:35; Romans 12:8; 2 Corinthians 8:3-4, 9-15; 9:6-15.

Source: Adapted from Evangelical Alliance, *Money For God's Sake* (Evangelical Alliance, 1993).

191. Treasure

(Antiques, Art, Outward appearance, Painting, Wealth)

In 1994, a woman brought an oil painting of some kittens along to the Antiques Roadshow for valuation. Her sister had recently bought it in a car boot sale for fifty pence: it wasn't in terribly good condition, and had actually acquired an extra scratch in the car on the way to the Roadshow. The expert immediately recognised it as the work of the Dutch artist Henrietta Ronner Knipp, and estimated its value at around £15,000!

Bible references: 1 Samuel 16:7; Matthew 13:44-6.

Source: BBC *Antiques Roadshow*.

192. Treasure

(Bequests, Outward appearance, Practical jokes, Wealth, Wills)

Dennis Tolam was an eighteenth-century resident of Cork who was thought to have salted away a considerable sum of money during his lifetime. His friends and relations were consequently extremely optimistic when they gathered to hear his will read out in 1769. Their hopes began to dwindle, however, as the old man's bequests were listed:

I leave to my sister-in-law four old stockings which will be found under my mattress, to the right.

To my nephew, Michael Tarles, two odd socks and a green nightcap.

To Lieutenant John Stein, a blue stocking with my red cloak.

To my cousin, Barbara Dolan, an old boot with a red flannel pocket.

To Hannah, my housekeeper, my broken water jug.

The disappointed heirs were about to leave the room, when Hannah, the old man's housekeeper, indignantly tossed the water jug onto the floor. It burst open to reveal a hoard of coins inside. As the others carefully examined the items they had been bequeathed, they, too, discovered that what they had taken to be a load of old tat in fact concealed Dennis Tolam's fortune!

Bible references: 1 Samuel 16:7; Matthew 13:44-6; 2 Corinthians 4:7.

Source: Adapted from *Tombstone Humour* (Chancellor Press, 1993), pp 147-8.

193. Wealth

(Disillusionment, Fame, Happiness, Power, Sex)

All he ever really wanted in life was more. He wanted more money, so he parlayed inherited wealth into a billion-dollar pile of assets. He wanted more fame, so he broke into the Hollywood scene and soon became a film-maker and star. He wanted more sensual pleasures, so he paid handsome sums to indulge his every sexual urge. He wanted more thrills, so he designed, built and piloted the fastest aircraft in the world. He wanted more power, so he secretly dealt political favours so skilfully that two US presidents became his pawns. All he ever wanted was more. He was absolutely convinced that more would bring him true satisfaction. Unfortunately, history shows otherwise.

He concluded his life emaciated and colourless, with a sunken chest, fingernails in grotesque, inches-long corkscrews, rotting black teeth, tumours, and innumerable needle marks from his drug addiction. Howard Hughes died believing the myth of more. He died a billionaire junkie, insane by all reasonable standards.

Bible references: Job 31:24-8; Psalm 49; 62:9-10; Proverbs 11:4, 28; Ecclesiastes 4:8; 5:10-19; Matthew 16:26; Mark 8:36; Luke 12:13-21; 1 Timothy 6:6-10, 17-19.

Source: Bill Hybels, in *Mastering Contemporary Preaching* (Multnomah Press, 1989), pp 119-20.

FAMOUS NAMES

194. Names

(Discipleship, History, Preaching, Puritans, Salvation, Humour)

The Puritans liked to follow the Old Testament custom of giving their children deeply meaningful (and sometimes very lengthy) names.

During the English Civil War there was a leatherseller named Praise-God Barebone, a self-appointed preacher who delivered a sermon lasting fully five hours to a congregation of about one hundred and fifty on a winter's afternoon. His two brothers bore names which were sermons in themselves, being called Christ-Came-Into-The-World-To-Save Barebone, and If-Christ-Had-Not-Died-Thou-Hadst-Been-Damned Barebone!

Towards the end of the sixteenth century, Puritan ministers were recorded in East Sussex named Fight-the-Good-Fight-of-Faith White (at Ewhurst), Safety-on-High Snat (in Uckfield) and Fly-Fornication Richardson (in Waldron).

Bible references: Genesis 17:5, 15; 25:25-6; 29:32-30:24;

202

35:10; Judges 6:32; Ruth 1:20; Isaiah 7:3, 14; 8:1; Jeremiah 20:3; Hosea 1:4-9; Matthew 1:21, 23.

Source: Adapted from Christopher Hibbert, *Cavaliers and Roundheads* (HarperCollins, 1993), p 28; Desmond Seward *Sussex* (Pimlico, 1995), p 120.

195. Royalty

(Accidents, Archbishops, Children, Duke of York, Prince of Wales, Sonship, Status, Humour)

One winter many years ago, the royal children in Buckingham Palace were looking out of the window when they saw some urchins playing in the snow. The governess had left them on their own, so they seized the opportunity, and slipping outside they got involved in a tremendous snowball fight. Unfortunately, as sometimes happens, a snowball smashed one of the palace windows, and almost immediately a soldier appeared and took the boys off to the guardroom. He turned to the first of the children and asked, 'What's your name, then, sonny?' 'Please sir,' came the reply, 'I'm the Prince of Wales.' The second said, 'If you please sir, I'm the Duke of York.' 'Oh you are, are you? And what about you, then?' he asked, turning to the third. The urchin wiped his nose on his sleeve and said, 'I'll stick wiv me mates, guv: I'm the Archbishop o' Canterbury.'

Bible references: Hosea 1:10; Matthew 5:9; John 1:12-13; Romans 8:14-17; Galatians 3:26; 4:4-7; Ephesians 1:5; 5:1; Hebrews 12:5-8; 1 John 3:1-2.

Source: Adapted from Daniel Cozens, Cambridge 1979.

196. Paul Azinger

(Cancer, Death, Faith, Heaven, Priorities, Sickness, Sport, Suffering, Testimony)

In 1993, the professional golfer Paul Azinger discovered that he had cancer of the shoulder. He had just won the American PGA tournament, his first major title. His initial reaction to the news was stunned disbelief, but when he saw a scan of the shoulder, he knew it was true. His commitment to Christianity had increased some years earlier when he and his wife Toni had been going through a difficult patch, but this was a real test to his faith.

His spiritual mentor, Larry Moody, the chaplain to the American golf tour, had once told him: 'Zinger, we're not in the land of the living going to the land of the dying; we're in the land of the dying trying to get to the land of the living.' Azinger commented: 'In a much deeper way than ever before, I began to understand what Larry was talking about.'

The cancer was successfully treated, but the experience changed the golfer's outlook in a profound and lasting way. On his return to the game he told a group of supporters, 'Even though it's great to be called a PGA Tour player, and it's probably greater to be called a PGA champion, I don't think there's any greater gift than the one that is mine, to be called a child of God because I place my trust in Jesus Christ. It is easy, even as a Christian, to be obsessed by where one is on the money list and tournament wins. This experience has been a reality check for me.'

'I know I will spend my eternity with God. And I have a

promise that as a child of God, he will help me deal with anything. He promises to give me that contentment no matter what life brings – even cancer.'

Bible references: Matthew 16:26; Mark 8:36; Luke 9:25; John 1:12-13; Romans 6:4-8; 8:11, 14-39; 2 Corinthians 4:16-18; Philippians 3:7-11; Colossians 3:1-4; 1 Peter 1:3-9.

Source: Adapted from reviews of Paul Azinger and Ken Abrahams, *Zinger* (HarperCollins, 1995), in the *Church of England Newspaper*, 11 August 1995 and 19 July 1996.

197. Thomas Edison

(Children, Expectations, Fathers, Inventions, Parents, Potential, School, Science, Sons, Success, Teachers, Work)

He was born in 1847 in Ohio, and said of his schooldays: 'I can remember that I never got on well at school. I was always bottom of the class. I always had the feeling that my teacher didn't like me, and that my father thought that I was stupid.' At the age of eight the teacher called him a dimwit in front of the rest of the class, so young Al ran out of the classroom and straight back home, where he vowed to his mother that he would never go to school again. He was as good as his word: he never attended another school, college or university.

At the age of twelve he got a job on the newly opened railways, selling fruit, nuts and sweets to the passengers. At fifteen he got hold of an old printing press, and began printing his own newspaper in the luggage van during the journey, with details of alterations to the timetable and other useful information. Although this was not to be the career path which he followed, it showed the inventive and entre-preneurial streak which was to mark him out in later life.

A few years later he developed his first invention: an electric rat trap. It was the first of more than 2,500 inventions which were to make Thomas Alva Edison a household name. These included the forerunner of the microphone, the phonograph, the earliest film camera and the electric light bulb. He also set up the world's first electric power station, in New York in 1882. Not bad for a boy who left school at eight!

Bible references: Proverbs 22:6; Ephesians 6:4; Colossians 3:21.

Source: Adapted from Gerhard Prause, *Genies in der Schule* (Econ Verlag, 1974), pp 253-5.

198. Jonathan Edwards

(Ambition, Commitment, Failure, Faith, Families, Persever-ance, Priorities, Sport, Success, Testimony)

In 1992, Jonathan Edwards nearly gave up athletics after failing to qualify for the final of the triple jump at the Barcelona Olympics. 'I don't think I've ever felt such pain and anguish,' he said. 'It had to be a bad dream. My whole future as an athlete seemed blown apart in just three awful jumps.' But failure taught him an invaluable lesson, which kept him going when others might have given up: 'God taught me again that my hope was to be in him, and not in happy circumstances, and that come what may, he is to be praised.'

The rest is history. At the World Championships in Gothenburg in 1995, Jonathan not only won gold with a world record jump, but went on to improve on that new record in his subsequent jumps. But even that experience didn't change this remarkable character, who said simply, 'Sometimes sport is given too much pre-eminence. There are many more important and serious issues in life.... The things that really matter to me are being a Christian, a husband and a family man.'

At the Olympics in 1996 he won the silver medal. Before the competition he was asked by fellow athlete and Christian Kriss Akabusi what would happen if he didn't win. He replied, 'I am an athlete, but first and foremost I am a Christian. My relationship with God cannot be affected by anything that happens at the Olympics. I don't know if it is God's will that I win. What is God's will for me is that I compete to the best of my ability and in whatever happens, I glorify him.'

Bible references: Matthew 16:26; Mark 8:36; Luke 9:25; Romans 8:28; 1 Corinthians 10:31; Philippians 3:7-9; Colossians 3:17.

Source: Adapted from *Challenge Newspaper*, Summer 1996; the *Church of England Newspaper*, 9 August 1996.

199. Benjamin Franklin

(Afterlife, Books, Death, Epitaph, Faith, History, Printing, Resurrection)

As a young printer in Philadelphia, Benjamin Franklin composed his own epitaph:

The Body of
B Franklin Printer
(Like the Cover of an old Book
Its Contents torn out
And stript of its Lettering and Gilding)
Lies here, Food for Worms.
But the Work shall not be lost;
For it will (as he believ'd) appear once more,
In a new and more elegant Edition
Revised and Corrected
By the Author.

Bible references: Job 19:26; John 3:16; 5:28-9; 6:40; 11:25-6; Romans 6:4-8; 8:11; 1 Corinthians 6:14; 15:22-3, 51-7; 1 Thessalonians 4:14-17.

Source: Quoted in Alister McGrath, *Roots that Refresh* (Hodder and Stoughton, 1992), p 126.

200. Adolf Hitler

(Children, Choirs, Church, Clergy, Expectations, Fathers, Parents, Potential, School, Singing, Sons, Teachers)

At the little school in Fischlam in Austria he was recognised as a good pupil, to the delight of his proud father, who was hoping that the lad would one day go on to become a civil servant. The schoolteacher later remembered him as 'mentally very much alert, obedient but lively.' When his report card came back, he had Grade 1s right across the board. His singing voice was naturally good, and on some afternoons he joined the choir at the local monastery.

At about the age of nine or ten, he became, in his own words, 'intoxicated' with that 'solemn splendour of brilliant church festivals.' He was a server at Mass, and the local abbot became his ideal. He later confided that as a small boy it was his most ardent wish to become a priest. He would drape the maid's apron around his shoulders, climb up on a kitchen chair and deliver long and fervent sermons.

As the boy grew older, things started to go sour. At secondary school his marks were not as good, and his behaviour provoked negative comment from his teachers. He himself wrote later that he was attempting to frustrate his father's plans: he didn't want to become a state official. But even after the sudden death of his father when the lad was only fourteen, his reports were merely 'satisfactory'; only in Drawing and Gymnastics did he do well.

As for his ideas about becoming a priest, these had long gone by the board. It is hard to say precisely when he turned against the church, but in later life, Adolf Hitler showed himself to be an enemy of the Christian faith rather than its friend; a persecutor rather than a protector.

Bible references: Proverbs 22:6; Ephesians 6:4; Colossians 3:21.

Source: Adapted from Gerhard Prause, *Genies in der Schule* (Econ Verlag, 1974), pp 36-8, and John Toland, *Adolf Hitler* (Doubleday, 1976), pp 8-12.

201. Adolf Hitler

(Christ, Counterfeit religion, Evil, False prophets, Jesus, Nazism, School, Unlikely Messiahs)

A textbook issued to German schools from 1934 taught them the following:

> As Jesus set men free from sin and hell, so Hitler rescued the German people from destruction. Both Jesus and Hitler were persecuted, but while Jesus was crucified, Hitler was exalted to Chancellor. While the disciples of Jesus betrayed their master and left him in his distress, the sixteen friends of Hitler stood by him. The apostles completed the work of their Lord. We hope that Hitler will lead his work to completion.

Bible references: Isaiah 14:13-15; Ezekiel 28:2; Matthew 24:23-4; Mark 13:22; Luke 21:8; 2 Thessalonians 2:4.

Source: Quoted in Edwin Robertson, *The Shame and the Sacrifice* (Hodder and Stoughton, 1987), p 89.

202. Martin Luther

(Conversion, Faith, Grace, History, Mercy, Reformation, Righteousness, Salvation, Testimony, Works)

Martin Luther's rediscovery of the doctrine of justification by faith changed the face of the church for ever. Here is his description, in his own words, of how it happened:

I was a good monk, and kept the rule of my order so strictly that I may say that if ever a monk got to heaven by his monkery, it was I.

I greatly longed to understand Paul's epistle to the Romans, but had been held up by one expression: 'the righteousness of God', which I had been taught to understand as the righteousness by which God is righteous and punishes unrighteous sinners. For my situation was this: however irreproachable my life as a monk, before God I felt myself to be a sinner with a troubled conscience, nor could I believe that my merit could appease him. So I did not love this righteous God who punishes sinners, but rather hated him and murmured against him. Yet I clung to dear Paul, and had a great yearning to know what he meant.

At last, as I meditated day and night, I saw the connection between the words 'the righteousness of God is revealed' and 'the righteous shall live by faith'. Then I grasped that the righteousness of God is that righteousness by which through grace and sheer mercy God makes us righteous through faith. At this I felt myself to be reborn and to have entered through open gates into paradise itself. There and then the whole of Scripture took on a new meaning, and whereas before 'the righteousness of God' had filled me with hate, now I began to love it and extol it as the sweetest word of all. This passage of Paul became to me a gate to heaven.

Bible references: Habakkuk 2:4; Romans 1:17; 3:21-8; 9:32; Galatians 3:10-14; Ephesians 2:8-9; Philippians 3:8-9.

Source: Adapted from Roland Bainton, *Here I Stand* (Lion, 1978), pp 45, 65.

203. Edvard Munch

(Art, Death, Grief, Mourning, Pain, Painting, Suffering)

The Norwegian artist Edvard Munch is best known for his painting *The Scream*, which former *Times* editor William Rees-Mogg has described as the perfect image to represent the twentieth century: hell on earth for billions of people.

But another of Munch's works, today in the National Gallery in Oslo, reveals even more poignantly the inner pain and anguish of the artist.

The painting is called *The Sick Child*, and it shows a pale red-headed girl gazing out of the window as her mother sits beside her, head bowed as if unable to look at her daughter. Behind the painting lies Munch's grief at losing his mother through tuberculosis when he was only five, and his beloved older sister Sophie when he was fourteen. With many paintings, it is best to stand back to appreciate the picture fully; with this one you need to go nearer. When you look closely at the picture, you see that it is scarred and furrowed by deep scratches scored across its surface, as if it has been carelessly handled or crudely vandalised. But neither is the case: it was Munch himself who made these marks, painting the image of the sick child and the faceless mother, then scratching them out, repainting them, scoring them out again, over and over, until the painting was so deeply marked that the scars remain visible to this day. These are the scars of bereavement, of grief, of the anguish in the artist's soul.

Bible references: 2 Samuel 1:17-27; 18:33; 2 Kings 13:14; John 11:33-6; Romans 12:15; 1 Thessalonians 4:13.

Source: Simon Coupland.

204. Napoleon III

(Death, Empire, Epitaphs, History, Human condition, Life, Obituaries)

The death certificate of the former French emperor Napoleon III can be found in Somerset House in London. One writer has called it 'the most poignant line ever entered across the columns of a ledger, a complete tragedy in three acts.' It is brutal in its succinctness, for what a story lies behind the few brief words.

Name: Napoleon.
Profession: Emperor of the French.
Cause of death: Exhaustion.

Bible references: Ecclesiastes 1:12-2:23.

Source: Quoted in the *Sunday Times*, 6 April 1986.

205. Pontius Pilate

(Crucifixion, Early Church, Jesus, New Testament, Saints)

The *Oxford Dictionary of Saints* doesn't list him, but one of the saints revered by the Ethiopian church is Pontius Pilate! As early as the third century, Tertullian claimed that the Roman governor was 'in his secret heart already a Christian', and that he had written a glowing account of Jesus to the Emperor. But by the fourth and fifth centuries the stories that were circulating about him portrayed Pilate as unwilling to condemn Jesus, and ultimately committing suicide when he realised the enormity of what he had done. Stories like this grew in the face of pagan attacks on Christianity, and ultimately led to the Ethiopian church recognising him as a saint.

Bible references: Matthew 27:11-26; Mark 15:1-15; Luke 23:1-25; John 18:28-19:22.

Source: Adapted from Alan Millard, *Discoveries from the Time of Jesus* (Lion, 1990), pp 68-9; Steve Mason, *Josephus and the New Testament* (Hendrickson, 1992), p 22.

206. The Duke of Wellington

(Administration, Commitment, History, Paperwork, Priorities, War, Humour)

The following witty if rather cutting letter was written by the Duke of Wellington to the Foreign Office during the Peninsular War in 1812:

Gentlemen,
    While marching from Portugal to a position which commands the approach to Madrid and the French forces, my officers have been diligently complying with your requests which have been sent by His Majesty's ship from London to Lisbon and thence by dispatch rider to our headquarters.

    We have enumerated our saddles, bridles, tents and poles, and all manner of sundry items for which His Majesty's government holds me accountable. I have dispatched reports on the character, wit and spleen of every officer. Each item and every farthing has been accounted for, with two regrettable exceptions for which I beg your indulgence.

Unfortunately, the sum of one shilling and ninepence remains unaccounted for in one infantry battalion's petty cash, and there has been a hideous confusion as to the number of jars of raspberry jam issued to one cavalry regiment during a sandstorm in Western Spain. This reprehensible carelessness may be related to the pressure of circumstance, since we are at war with France, a fact which may come as a bit of a surprise to you gentlemen in Whitehall.

This brings me to my present purpose, which is to request elucidation of my instructions from His Majesty's government, so that I may better understand why I am dragging an army over these barren plains. I construe that perforce it must be one of two alternative duties, as given below. I shall pursue either one with the best of my ability but I cannot do both.

1) To train an army of uniformed British clerks in Spain for the benefit of the accountants and copy-boys in London, or perchance
2) To see to it that the forces of Napoleon are driven out of Spain.

Your most obedient servant,

Wellington

Bible references: 1 Samuel 15:22; Psalm 51:16-17; Isaiah 1:11-17; Jeremiah 7:21-6; Amos 5:21-4; Micah 6:6-8; Matthew 23:23-4; Luke 11:42.

Source: Quoted by George Carey, Evangelical Anglican Leaders' Conference, 7 January 1995.

CHRISTMAS AND EASTER

207. Christmas – Incarnation

(Christ, Fishing, Humility, Husbands, Poverty, Quarrels, Wives, Wealth)

There was once a poor peasant family, so poor that one day they found themselves with literally nothing left to eat for supper. So the wife sent the man out to fish, telling him that unless he caught something they would go hungry that night. The man fished and fished, and at last got a bite. It was a whopper, and after a hard struggle he eventually managed to land it. He was about to bring down his club when, to his astonishment, the fish spoke. 'Don't kill me!' it said. 'If you throw me back I'll grant you three wishes – whatever you ask.' Well, the man thought this sounded marvellous, so he tossed the fish back in the water and rushed home to tell his wife.

'Where's the supper then?' she shouted as she saw him running up empty-handed. 'You lazy good-for-nothing, didn't you catch anything?' So her husband explained how he'd caught a talking fish, and thrown it back because it had told him it would grant him three wishes. 'What a lot of nonsense!' his wife exclaimed. 'You're making it up because you couldn't catch anything.' 'I'm not!' he answered. 'Here, I'll prove it! I wish – I wish we had supper on the table.' And at once – hey presto! – a meal appeared on their table.

'You stupid man!' cried his wife. 'We've only got three wishes and you've wasted the first one already! Why, you could have asked for anything, a new home or whatever we liked!'

'Right then,' said her husband, and before she could stop him he went on, 'I wish we had a new home.' And again, in an instant the house was transformed.

'You stupid, stupid man!' the wife shouted again. 'Don't say anything else! We could do much better than this house. I wish we had a palace fit for a king, no, wait, fit for God himself to live in!' And at once they found themselves standing in a dark, dirty, poky little stable with a manger on the wall and straw on the floor.

Bible references: Matthew 20:28; Mark 10:45; Luke 2:1-16; John 1:1-14; 13:3-12; 2 Corinthians 8:9; Philippians 2:5-11; Hebrews 5:8.

Source: Adapted from *Making the Most of Christmas* (CPAS, 1992), p 18.

208. Christmas – Nativity plays

(Angels, Children, Epiphany, Magi, Misunderstanding, School, Virgin birth, Humour)

At a school in Derby, three six-year-olds were playing the wise men in the school nativity play. As they came up to

Mary and Joseph at the stable, the first one handed over his present and said, 'Gold.' The second presented his gift and said, 'Myrrh.' The third one then gave them his treasure and said, 'And Frank sent this.'

At another school, two little girls were talking about their roles in the nativity play. 'I'm going to be a virgin,' one announced smugly. 'That's nothing,' replied the other, 'I'm going to be an angel.' 'Well my mummy says it's much harder to be a virgin,' retorted the first.

Bible references: Matthew 1:18-2:12; Luke 1:26-38; 2:1-20; John 1:13.

Source: Adapted from the *Daily Telegraph*, 10 January 1983, and the *Church of England Newspaper*, May 1996.

209. Christmas – Observance

(Church, Church-going, Food, History, Holidays, Law, Sport)

Over the centuries, the Church has tried to ensure that Christmas remains a holy festival rather than a secular feast, with varying degrees of success. For instance, an act passed by Oliver Cromwell's Long Parliament in 1644 – and never subsequently repealed – describes Christmas pudding and mince pies as 'abominable and idolatrous things to be avoided by all Christians'. The law goes on to state that everyone must 'observe the monthly fast' on 'the Feast of the Nativitie of Our Saviour'.

An earlier statute, the Holy Days and Fasting Act of 1551, stipulates to this day that everyone must attend a church service on Christmas Day, and also specifies that they must walk there and back.

As for what we do during the holiday, the 1541 Unlawful Games Act with its subsequent amendments makes it clear that even now the only sports permitted on Christmas Day are archery, leaping and vaulting. This was underlined in 1625 by an act which laid down: 'There shall be no meetings, assemblings or concourse of people out of their owne parishes for any sports or pastimes whatsoever.'

Bible references: Mark 7:18-19; Acts 10:15; Romans 14:1-6, 13-23; Galatians 4:10; Colossians 2:16, 20-3; 1 Timothy 4:3-5.

Source: Adapted from the *Daily Telegraph*, 24 December 1996.

210. Christmas – Santa Claus

(Agnostics, the Devil, Dyslexia, God, Unbelief, Humour)

The joke is by now well known: What does a dyslexic insomniac agnostic do at night? Answer: he lies awake and wonders whether there's a Dog. Perhaps less familiar is a Christmas variation: Did you hear about the dyslexic devil worshipper who sold his soul to Santa?

Source: the *Church of England Newspaper*, 12 January 1996.

211. Christmas – Sermons

(Army, Chaplains, Church, Clergy, Missionaries, Preaching, Humour)

The vicar climbed, with some effort, into the pulpit. He was an elderly man who had served in India most of his life…. His sermons had been composed in his more active days for delivery at the garrison chapel; he had done nothing to adapt them to the changed conditions of his ministry and they mostly concluded with some reference to homes and dear ones far away. The villagers did not find this in any way surprising. Few of the things said in church seemed to have any particular reference to themselves. They enjoyed their vicar's sermons very much and they knew that when he began about their distant homes, it was time to be dusting their knees and feeling for their umbrellas….

The vicar preached his usual Christmas sermon. It was one to which his parishioners were greatly attached. 'How difficult it is for us,' he began, blandly surveying his congregation, who coughed into their mufflers and chafed their chilblains under their woollen gloves, 'to realise that this is indeed Christmas. Instead of the glowing log fire and windows tight shuttered against the drifting snow, we have only the harsh glare of an alien sun; instead of the happy circle of loved faces, of home and family, we have the uncomprehending stares of the subjugated, though no doubt grateful, heathen. Instead of the placid ox and ass of Bethlehem,' said the vicar, slightly losing the thread of his comparisons, 'we have for companions the ravening tiger and the exotic camel, the furtive jackal and the ponderous elephant…'. And so on, through the pages of faded manuscript.

Bible references: Matthew 1:18-2:12; Luke 1-2.

Source: Evelyn Waugh, *A Handful of Dust* (Penguin, 1951), pp 32, 60.

212. Christmas – Virgin birth

(Aliens, Belief, End times, Eschatology, Gullibility, Insurance, Second Coming, Humour)

Some 300 British women have taken out insurance against having a virgin birth by an act of God. The policy, offered by London insurance brokers Goodfellow Rebecca Ingrams Pearson, promises to pay out £1 million in the event of a virgin birth – to be verified by an independent panel of gynaecologists – against an annual payment of £100. Nearly 300 women took up the policy in the first fortnight after it was launched, a number of them from an exclusively female sect who reportedly believed that this would hasten the return of Christ. The managing director, Simon Burgess, said, 'Women from eighteen-year-olds to pensioners have taken out the policy. It is a genuine issue for them. They want a Second Coming to happen – and so they're tempting fate.'

This is the not the company's only unusual policy – a scheme insuring against impregnation by aliens was taken up by 723 people in just four weeks. Mr Burgess commented, 'You must never underestimate the stupidity of the British public. We're getting more interest from virgins and people who believe in aliens than people who will take out a policy that is likely to pay off.'

Bible references: Isaiah 7:14; Matthew 1:18-25; Luke 1:30-5; John 1:12-13.

Source: Adapted from the *Daily Telegraph*, September 1996.

213. Easter – the Cross

(Atonement, Christ, Doctor, Medicine, Missionaries, Sacrifice, Sickness, Suffering)

A young man went out to China to serve as a missionary doctor. He was soon sent inland because of sickness among the more senior staff, and found himself on his own in an isolated hospital with little knowledge of the language. To his horror, a terrible epidemic then broke out in the region. He was still too inexperienced in tropical diseases to diagnose the sickness, let alone treat it. What he needed was advice from Shanghai, but none of his patients would survive the journey. If only he had someone who was newly infected, there was a chance that they could reach Shanghai and allow the more experienced doctors there to diagnose the illness.

So he took blood from one of his infected patients and injected it into his own veins before setting off for Shanghai. He took their sickness upon himself so that they might be healed. In effect, he laid down his life that they might live.

Bible references: Isaiah 53:4-7; Matthew 20:28; 26:26-8; Mark 10:45; 14:22-4; Luke 22:19-20; John 3:14-17; Romans 4:25; 5:6-11; 8:1-4; 1 Corinthians 5:7; 15:3; 2 Corinthians 5:14-15; 1 Thessalonians 5:10; 1 Timothy 2:5-6; Titus 2:14; Hebrews 9:15, 28; 1 Peter 1:18-19; 2:24-5; 3:18.

Source: Adapted from Arnold Aldis, in William Purcell, *Seekers and Finders* (Mowbray, 1985).

214. Easter – the Cross

(Atonement, Chaplains, Clergy, Commitment, Sacrifice, War)

During the Second World War, an RAF bomber flying a mission over Germany was hit by flak. Several of the crew were wounded, and the aircraft was badly damaged, and losing height all too fast. The one uninjured person in the body of the plane was an RAF chaplain who had accompanied the flight, so the pilot called back to him to throw out as much baggage as he could to keep the aircraft flying. Out went everything that the padre could lay his hands on, even the fire extinguishers and in the end the parachutes, but still the plane was losing height, and the pilot could see a range of hills ahead which they were barely going to clear. As the peaks came nearer and nearer the plane lurched upwards, almost scraped the ground, but just managed to clear the treetops. In the distance the pilot could now see the English channel, and shouted out, 'Padre, we've made it!' But there was no reply. The pilot called several more times before he realised that the chaplain was no longer there. He had thrown himself out of the aircraft to give it that last bit of height it needed to clear the hills. He had sacrificed his life so that the rest of the crew could live.

Bible references: Isaiah 53:4-7; Matthew 20:28; 26:26-8; Mark 10:45; 14:22-4; Luke 22:19-20; John 3:14-17; Romans 4:25; 5:6-11; 8:1-4; 1 Corinthians 5:7; 15:3; 2 Corinthians 5:14-15; 1 Thessalonians 5:10; 1 Timothy 2:5-6; Titus 2:14; Hebrews 9:15, 28; 1 Peter 1:18-19; 2:24-5; 3:18.

Source: Adapted from Daniel Cozens, Cambridge, 27 May 1979.

215. Easter – the Cross

(Commitment, Death, Discipleship, Faith, Jesus, Life, Priorities)

Admiral Richard Byrd led four expeditions to the Antarctic, including one in 1933, when he studied the polar night, which lasts for four long dark months. At one stage he left his hut for a walk outside, but when he turned round he could no longer see its familiar shape. The falling snow had already obliterated his footsteps. The polar cold cut through his clothing; if he failed to find the hut soon, he would surely die in the endless Arctic snow.

He had with him a long staff which he had been using to keep his footing. Now he drove it into the icy ground and said to himself, 'I know the hut isn't far off. If I always keep this staff in sight, I can try out different directions until I see the hut.' Several attempts failed before at last he regained the hut. The crucial thing was that he had never taken his eyes off his staff. For him, that reference point meant the difference between life and death.

Bible references: Psalm 25:15; 123:2; John 3:14-21; 6:40; 12:32-6; 19:37; 1 Corinthians 2:2; Hebrews 12:2-3.

Source: Adapted from Colin Whittaker, in *Alpha* magazine, April 1992.

216. Easter – Crucifixion

(Ancient history, the Cross, Death, Jesus, Roman Empire, Suffering)

The Roman writer Seneca (c. 4 BC–AD 65) provides us with a unique contemporary description of the utter horror of death by crucifixion. He writes not as a Christian, but as a horrified observer of the suffering inflicted by this barbarous form of execution:

> Can anyone be found who would prefer wasting away in pain dying limb by limb, or letting out his life drop by drop, rather than expiring once for all? Can any man be found willing to be fastened to the accursed tree, long sickly, already deformed, swelling with ugly weals on shoulders and chest, and drawing the breath of life amid long-drawn-out agony? He would have many excuses for dying even before mounting the cross.

Bible references: Psalm 22; Isaiah 53; Matthew 16:24-5; 20:19; 26:2; 27:32-50; Mark 8:34-5; 15:21-37; Luke 9:23-4; 24:26-46; John 19:16-37; 1 Corinthians 1:18-24; 2 Corinthians 13:4; Galatians 3:13; 6:14; Philippians 2:6-8; Hebrews 12:2.

Source: Quoted in Martin Hengel, *The Cross of the Son of God* (SCM, 1986), pp 122-3.

217. Easter – Resurrection

(Animals, Belief, Evidence, Faith, Miracles, Unbelief)

In the late eighteenth century, reports began to filter back from eastern Australia of the discovery of a bizarre new creature. It was a furry mammal roughly the size of a rabbit, but it had webbed feet and a bill like a duck. Most extraordinary of all, it was said to reproduce itself by laying eggs, unlike any other mammal. The duck-billed platypus, as the creature was named, was so utterly unlike any other known creature that even when the first skin was sent back to Europe, many zoologists regarded it as a hoax.

It wasn't until 1884, when a female platypus was shot just after laying an egg, and found to have another egg still inside her body, that the experts finally had to concede that the duck-billed platypus really was unique – an egg-laying mammal.

The problem with the platypus was that it contradicted people's presuppositions. Rather than admit they were wrong and change their theories, they preferred to dismiss it, despite the wealth of evidence in its favour. It's the same with the resurrection. Many people are unwilling to take the evidence seriously, because to admit that it actually happened would be too challenging, and too demanding.

Bible references: Matthew 28:1-10, 17; Mark 16:1-8; Luke 1:1-4; 16:30-1; 24:1-43; John 20:1-31; 21:24; Acts 1:1-3; 2:24, 32; 13:30-7; 17:31-2; Romans 1:3-4; 1 Corinthians 15:1-8, 12-20; 1 Peter 1:21.

Source: Adapted from Ross Clifford, *Leading Lawyers Look at the Resurrection* (Albatross Books, 1991), pp 104-5.

218. Easter – Resurrection

(Belief, Christianity, the Cross, Counterfeit religion, Crucifixion, Faith, History, Jesus, Religion)

Talleyrand, one of the leading figures in the French Revolution, was reportedly approached by a friend one day who wanted his advice. The friend told Talleyrand that he had been trying to win support for a new religion which he himself had invented. He claimed that in philosophical terms, the new religion was a marked improvement on Christianity, but he was finding it extremely difficult to create popular interest. What should he do?

Talleyrand thought for a moment. He agreed that the difficulties were formidable, and he found it hard to know what to advise. 'Still,' he mused, 'there is one plan which you might at least try. I suggest you get yourself crucified and then rise again on the third day!'

Source: Quoted in Scripture Union *SALT* material April-June 1995, from John Young, *The Case Against Christ*.

219. Easter – Secularised

(Church-going, Modern life, Religion, Unbelief, the World)

Someone in a Weymouth bookshop overheard the following complaint from a teenage girl trying to choose an Easter card with her mother. 'Oh no, Mum, not a religious one. They're bad enough at Christmas.' A similar attitude could be found in Merseyside, where a church member gave a copy of their newsletter to a parishioner. 'Fancy that, St Andrew's,' said the man, 'Haven't been there for years.' 'Why not come along at Easter?' asked the distributor. 'You'll be very welcome.' 'Easter?' came the reply. 'Why, is there something special on?'

Source: Adapted from the *Daily Telegraph*, 1980 and 23 March 1989.

MISTAKES AND MISUNDERSTANDINGS

220. Accidents

(Baptism, Clergy, Death, Electricity, Microphones, Mistakes, Humour)

An elderly Swedish pastor met a most unfortunate end during the winter of 1955. Pastor Karlo Toivio was about to baptise some new members of his church by total immersion, and was standing ready in the baptism tank, up to his waist in water. Things went terribly wrong when his assistant handed him a live microphone.

Source: Adapted from *Tombstone Humour* (Chancellor Press, 1993), p 269.

221. Baptism

(Children, Clergy, Mistakes, Names, Sacraments, Humour)

An old rector grew ever more exasperated by the custom of giving a child a string of fancy-sounding names. One day, when his customary enquiry to 'Name this child' was yet again answered by a number of fine-sounding names, his patience finally snapped. 'I'll have no more of these fine names,' he fulminated. 'I shall christen it plain John.' He regretted his rashness afterwards, when it was pointed out to him in the vestry that the child had in fact been a girl.

Source: Adapted from P. H. Ditchfield, *The Old-time Parson*, quoted in A. N. Wilson (ed.) *The Faber Book of Church and Clergy* (Faber and Faber, 1992), p 157.

222. Baptism

(Army, Church, Language, Liturgy, Misunderstanding, Parents, Translation, Humour)

One Sunday, a group of thirty Royal Marines who were on a posting in Norway went to the local church. Their Norwegian was limited, and the Lutherans seemed to sit down and stand up at different times from those they were used to, so they followed the cue given by the locals. The pastor gave an address, and at the end asked a question. A man at the front stood up, so all the marines followed suit. Fellow worshippers laughed, and explained to the men afterwards that what the pastor had asked was, 'Will the father of the child who is to be christened on Monday please stand up?'

Source: Adapted from the *Daily Telegraph*, 26 October 1993.

223. Computers

(Bible, Mistakes, Science, Technology, Translation, Humour)

Some years ago, the first computer programme was created to translate English into Russian. Years of research and development had gone into the project, and thousands of words, phrases and grammatical rules had been programmed into the machine. At last the day came: the work was finished. One of the scientists was given the honour of typing in the first sentence to be translated, so he chose one from the Bible: 'The spirit is willing, but the flesh is weak.' A few moments later the computer came up with the translation: 'The vodka is good, but the meat is off.'

Bible references: Matthew 26:41; Mark 14:38.

Source: unknown.

224. Misprints

(Advertisements, Mistakes, Misunderstandings, Newspapers, Relationships, Humour)

The following series of small ads reportedly appeared in the classified section of a small-town daily newspaper in the United States, showing how sometimes trying to make things better only makes them worse.

(Monday) FOR SALE. R. D. Jones has one sewing machine for sale. Phone 555-0707 after 7pm and ask for Mrs Kelly who lives with him cheap.

(Tuesday) NOTICE. We regret having erred in R. D. Jones's ad. yesterday. It should have read: One sewing machine for sale. Cheap: 555-0707 and ask for Mrs Kelly who lives with him after 7pm.

(Wednesday) NOTICE. R. D. Jones has informed us that he has received several annoying telephone calls because of the error we made in his classified ad. yesterday. His ad. stands corrected as follows: FOR SALE – R.D. Jones has one sewing machine for sale. Cheap. Phone 555-0707 and ask for Mrs Kelly who loves with him.

(Thursday) NOTICE. I, R. D. Jones, have NO sewing machine for sale. I SMASHED IT. Don't call 555-0707, as the telephone has been disconnected. I have NOT been carrying on with Mrs Kelly. Until yesterday she was my housekeeper, but she quit.

Source: Quoted in Barbara Johnson, *Splashes of Joy in the Cesspools of Life* (Word, 1992), p 115.

225. Missing the point

(Books, Countryside, Gamekeeping, Literature, Reviews, Humour)

The following unfortunate review of *Lady Chatterley's Lover* once appeared in the American magazine *Field and Stream*:

Although written many years ago, *Lady Chatterley's Lover* has just been reissued by the Grove Press, and this pictorial account of the day-to-day life of an English gamekeeper is full of considerable interest to outdoor minded readers, as it contains many passages on pheasant-raising, the apprehending of poachers, ways to control vermin, and other chores and duties of the professional gamekeeper. Unfortunately one is obliged to wade through many pages of extraneous material in order to discover and savour those sidelights on the management of a Midland shooting estate, and in this reviewer's opinion the book cannot take the place of J R Miller's *Practical Gamekeeping*.

Source: *Field and Stream* magazine.

226. Misunderstanding

(Accidents, Dancing, Electricity, Husbands, Marriage, Music, Wives, Humour)

A woman came home to find her husband frantically shaking and vibrating round the kitchen with what looked like a wire running from his waist towards the electric kettle. Thinking he was suffering an electric shock, she smashed a heavy piece of wood into him to jolt him away from the electric current, breaking his arm in two places. It was only then that she discovered he was dancing while listening to his Walkman.

Source: *The Southport, Ormskirk and Formby Star*, quoted in Scripture Union *SALT* material April-June 1995.

227. Names

(Advertisements, Dogs, Luck, Misfortune, Humour)

The following notice once appeared on the small ads board in a grocery store:

LOST. Dog with three legs, blind in left eye, missing right ear, tail broken and recently castrated. Answers to the name of 'Lucky.'

Bible references: Genesis 17:5; 25:25-6; 32:28; 1 Samuel 4:21; Ruth 1:20; Jeremiah 20:3.

Source: Quoted in Barbara Johnson, *Stick a Geranium in Your Hat and Be Happy!* (Word, 1990), p 1.

228. Numbers

(Dreams, Failure, Gambling, Horse racing, Luck, Misfortune, Prediction, Superstition, Humour)

A man who was due to go the races at Haydock one Saturday kept dreaming for several nights beforehand of the number seven. Being a superstitious man, he decided to act on this premonition. He scraped together all the money he could possibly afford and set off to the course. He waited until the seventh race, and put the whole lot on horse number seven. His premonition came true, even beyond his expectations. The horse, whose name was Haywire, finished seventh.

Bible references: Genesis 41:1-7, 17-32; Joshua 6:4; 2 Kings 5:10, 14; Matthew 22:25-8; Revelation 1:20; 4:5; 5:1, 5:6; 8:2; 15:1.

Source: Adapted from Michael Green, *The Peterborough Book* (Sphere, 1982), p 13.

229. Parable

(Bible, Jesus, Mistakes, Stories, Students, Humour)

Sometimes people get their Bible stories very confused, as this mixed-up parable, supposedly told by a first year entering an American college, reveals.

Once upon a time, a man went down from Jerusalem to Jericho and fell among thieves. And the thorns grew up and choked that man. And he went on and met the Queen of Sheba, and she gave that man a thousand talents of gold and silver, and a hundred changes of raiment. And he got in his chariot and drove furiously, and as he was driving under a big tree his hair got caught in a limb and left him hanging there.

And he hung there many days and many nights, and the ravens brought him food to eat and water to drink. And one night while he was hanging there asleep, his wife Delilah came along and cut his hair. And he dropped and fell on stony ground. And it began to rain, and it rained forty days and forty nights. And he hid himself in a cave. And he went out and met a man and said, 'Come and take supper with me in my cave.' But the man answered, 'I cannot, for I have married a wife.' And the cave-dweller went out into the highways and byways and compelled people to come in.

And he went on and came to Jericho and he saw Queen Jezebel sitting high up in a window and when she saw him, she laughed. And he said, 'Throw her down!' He said,

'Throw her down' again. And they threw her down seventy times seven. And of the fragments they picked up twelve baskets. And now, what I want to know is, whose wife will she be on the day of resurrection?

Bible references: Genesis 7:12; Judges 16:19; 2 Samuel 15:1; 18:9; 1 Kings 10:1-2, 10; 17:6; 19:9; 2 Kings 9:30-3; Matthew 13:5, 7, 10-15, 34-5; 18:22; 22:28; Mark 4:10-12, 33-4; Luke 8:9-10; 14:16-21; John 6:13.

Source: Quoted in Barbara Johnson, *Splashes of Joy in the Cesspools of Life* (Word, 1992), p 116.

230. Philosophy

(Disillusionment, Mistakes, Religion, Truth)

The influential philosopher A. J. Ayer was being interviewed by Brian Magee when he was asked the question: 'Logical positivism must have had real defects. What do you now, in retrospect, think the main ones were?' Without hesitation, Ayer replied, 'Well, I suppose the most important of the defects was that nearly all of it was false.'

Bible references: Isaiah 59:4-15; Romans 1:25; 2 Timothy 4:3-4; 2 Peter 2:16.

Source: Quoted in Church of England Doctrine Commission, *We Believe in God*, p 20.

231. Second Coming

(Church, Dishonesty, Disillusionment, End times, Eschatology, False prophets, Mistakes, Money, Sects, Stealing)

In 1992, a South Korean church leader named Lee Jang Rim persuaded 20,000 followers that the Rapture would occur on 28 October of that year. To prepare themselves for the Lord's coming, people abandoned their jobs and their education, sold their homes, divorced their spouses and deserted the army. Some women are even reported to have had abortions so that they wouldn't be too heavy to be lifted up to heaven! In all, these gullible followers gave over $4 million to Lee and his church.

As the midnight deadline approached, the South Korean government sent 1,500 riot police to Lee's 'Mission for the Coming Days', and placed the fire and ambulance services on alert. As it was, the deadline passed uneventfully, and next day forty-six-year-old Lee apologised to his followers for misleading them, and dissolved his church. The authorities were unimpressed, however, and sentenced the prophet to two years' imprisonment for fraud and illegal possession of US currency. The prosecution successfully argued that if Lee truly believed what he preached, what was he doing holding bank bonds which would only reach maturation in May 1993?

Bible references: Matthew 24:3-44; 25:1-13; Mark 13:3-37; Luke 12:35-46; 17:20-37; 21:8-9; John 14:3; Acts 1:11; 1 Thessalonians 4:16-5:4; 2 Peter 3:10-13; Revelation 22:7, 12, 20.

Source: Adapted from Russell Chandler, *Doomsday* (Word, 1993), pp 261-2.

232. Trustworthiness

(Accidents, Death, Dishonesty, Epitaphs, Failure, Promises, Humour)

In Girard cemetery in Pennsylvania is the following memorial:

> In memory of
> ELLEN SHANNON
> Who was fatally burned by the
> explosion of a lamp filled with
> Danforth's Non-Explosive Fluid

Bible references: Jeremiah 5:12-13; 14:13-16; 23:16-17; 27:9-15; Amos 9:10; Micah 3:11; Matthew 7:16-20; 12:33; Luke 6:43-44; James 3:12.

Source: Quoted in *Tombstone Humour* (Chancellor Press, 1993), p 31.

233. Wedding

(Best man, Bridegroom, Marriage, Mistakes, Humour)

In the little church of Kileter in County Tyrone in Ireland in the 1920s, Albert Muldoon was the best man at his friend's wedding. He walked up to the altar with him to await the arrival of the bride, but by an unfortunate oversight, stood on the groom's left instead of his right.

The bride arrived, the ceremony began, and when it came to the priest's questions, he asked them of the man standing next to the bride, and Albert duly answered them. As the service ended, the priest asked the newly-weds to sign the register. It was only at this point that the bridegroom plucked up the courage to say something, asking the priest whether, as the groom, he shouldn't be the one to sign. As soon as the priest found out what had happened, he led the bridal party back to the altar and took the wedding all over again, this time with the bridegroom and the best man the right way round.

Albert said afterwards, 'My pal, Christopher, the bridegroom, was so nervous that he didn't seem able to speak, so I thought I had better answer for him.'

Bible references: Genesis 29:16-27; Judges 15:1-2.

Source: Adapted from Nigel Blundell, *The World's Greatest Mistakes* (Hamlyn, 1991), pp 24-5.

ALTERNATIVES

234. Astrology

(Belief, Gullibility, Horoscopes, Prediction, Psychology)

One reason for the popularity of horoscopes is, according to Dr Susan Blackmore, senior lecturer in psychology at the University of the West of England in Bristol, because people want to feel more in control of their lives. 'We live in an uncertain world. We want to be able to predict the future, to regain our sense of control. And it does not always matter if that control is spurious or valid.' Dr Blackmore continued, 'It is interesting that those who turn to astrology tend to be those with least control over their own lives, which may be why horoscopes are more common in women's magazines.'

Professor Adrian Furnham of University College London offered another reason for astrology's appeal: what he calls the fallacy of personal validation. This means that people seize on something in the broad, generalised and trite words of the horoscope and relate it to themselves. After almost four decades of psychological research into the subject, Professor Furnham suggested four simple rules to write your own horoscope:

● Use double-headed, catch-all phrases, such as 'On the outside you are confident, but deep down you are insecure'.

● Be tantalisingly vague: 'You have an unfulfilled ambition'; 'This is a time of great soul-searching'.

● Include some pseudo science: 'Mars is adversely affected by Pluto'; 'The Sun flounces into Aquarius'.

● Tell people what they want to hear: 'The position of the Sun will give you the courage to sort out your career'; 'Channel your anger to change something you care about'.

Our brain subconsciously aids the horoscope industry, because we are programmed to spot the one prediction which is true among thousands which miss the mark; and that is the one we remember. 'The human mind is made for connections, and people will look for them in everything,' said Susan Blackmore. 'This is what makes us able to understand the world, and what trips us up when we read significance into horoscopes.' Studies of the accuracy of astrological predictions have revealed 'no correlations worth speaking of'. The only instance where small correlations have been found is among people who take notice of their horoscopes, a trend of concern to Dr Blackmore. 'People have been conforming to what they think their star signs are saying,' she said. 'I think that is really alarming, that people are distorting their natural personality to conform to expectations.'

Bible references: Genesis 1:16; Deuteronomy 4:19; 17:2-5; 2 Kings 21:1-5; 23:4-5; Psalm 8:3; 33:6, 136:7-9, 147:4; Isaiah 40:26; 44:24-5; 45:12; 47:13-15; Jeremiah 8:2; 31:35; Daniel 2:1-12; 4:7; 5:7-8; Zephaniah 1:4-6; Matthew 2:1-2; James 1:17.

Source: Adapted from the *Daily Telegraph*, 21 January 1995.

235. Astrology

(Belief, Gullibility, Horoscopes, Personality)

In 1968 a French magazine carried the following advertisement:

> ABSOLUTELY FREE!
> Your ultra-personal horoscope
> A TEN-PAGE DOCUMENT
> Benefit from a unique experiment
> Send name, address, date and place of birth to:
> ASTRAL ELECTRONIC

The first 150 respondents from the many who replied were then sent a ten-page character analysis, along with a questionnaire which asked them to identify how accurate they felt the profile to be. Unbeknown to them, the horoscopes were not based on the individual birth details which they had sent in, but were all identical. What was more, the horoscope which they received, which had been drawn up by one of the country's leading astrologers, was based on the birth in Auxerre at 3 am on 17 January 1897 of Dr Marcel Petiot, France's Dr Crippen, who at his trial claimed to have murdered sixty-three people!

The remarkable thing is that no fewer than 94 per cent of those who returned their questionnaires said that they recognised themselves in the psychological portraits. And fully 90 per cent said that their families and friends endorsed that view.

Bible references: Genesis 1:16; Deuteronomy 4:19; 17:2-5; 2 Kings 21:1-5; 23:4-5; Psalm 8:3; 33:6; 136:7-9; 147:4; Isaiah 40:26; 44:24-5; 45:12; 47:13-15; Jeremiah 8:2; 31:35; Daniel 2:1-12; 4:7; 5:7-8; Zephaniah 1:4-6; Matthew 2:1-2; James 1:17.

Source: Adapted from the *Daily Telegraph*, 15 September 1984, and Colin Chapman, *Shadows of the Supernatural* (Lion, 1990), p 132.

236. Astrology

(Accidents, Belief, Bondage, Conversion, Fear, Freedom, Healing, Horoscopes, Liberation, Prediction, Superstition)

Flossie was a sweet-natured lady of seventy who had been housebound for many years. But the reason for her confinement at home was not physical but psychological. It was agoraphobia that kept her indoors, and it was reading her horoscope that had led to her agoraphobia.

She had regularly read her horoscope, but had always said, like so many people, 'I only read them for fun. I mean, they don't really work, do they?' Until the fateful day when her horoscope had warned her not to go out, as it could be dangerous. Dismissing it as usual, Flossie went out – and met with a minor accident. From that day on, Flossie blamed herself for not heeding the warning she had been given, and became a prisoner to what 'her stars' told her. Unless the column actually said that she should go out, she remained at home, and in the end was diagnosed as suffering from agoraphobia.

Happily, Flossie met some caring Christians who told her about the love and power of Jesus, and she gradually began to rebuild her life. In time, she started to go out again, freed from the constraints which the horoscopes had placed around her. Progress was slow, but at last she was starting to live again.

Bible references: Genesis 1:16; Deuteronomy 4:19; 17:2-5; 2 Kings 21:1-5; 23:4-5; Psalm 8:3; 33:6; 136:7-9; 147:4; Isaiah 40:26; 44:24-5; 45:12; 47:13-15; Jeremiah 8:2, 31:35; Daniel 2:1-12; 4:7; 5:7-8; Zephaniah 1:4-6; Matthew 2:1-2; James 1:17.

Source: Adapted from Audrey Harper, 'Deliverance means love', *Renewal*, February 1993.

237. Cults – CBJ

(Afterlife, Counterfeit religion, Death, Eternity, Gullibility, Human nature, Immortality, Life, New Age)

Many religious groups promise their followers eternal life, but CBJ is undoubtedly one of the more bizarre. Founded in 1968 and based in Scottsdale, Arizona, CBJ has attracted a widespread following in America's wealthy, health-conscious West Coast, and boasts a mailing list of some 30,000 people in eighteen countries, including England.

CBJ was the brainchild of Charles Brown, BernaDeane (who doesn't use a last name) and James Strole: hence the name. 'It's not intelligent to die,' said BernaDeane, who was a fashion model before she became immortal. 'It's embarrassing to die.' Her husband Charles, a former nightclub singer and Assemblies of God pastor, would get annoyed with critics who asked why, if he can regenerate his own cells, he needed to wear a wig. James, who used to be a property salesman, said, 'Let the world prove to me that a human being has to die. We see them dying, sure, but that doesn't prove they have to die. It doesn't mean a damn thing.'

The idea behind CBJ is simple. 'We're waking the

immortal gene within us,' Charles explained, 'to where it becomes the predominant gene in the body, and consumes the genetics that accept that death is inevitable.' Devotees would hug and chant to 'awaken their cells' before moving on to 'cellular intercourse', during which their cells would 'penetrate' and 'impregnate' their fellows with immortality. Of course, eternal life isn't cheap: CBJ netted an estimated £1.3 million in 1993. A visit to the group's annual 'convergence' in Scottsdale, for instance, cost around £560 per head.

Critics asked why some members of CBJ had died since the group was established. BernaDeane had an answer ready: 'There probably was not enough energy together. They had not come to a place within their own self, and with others.' Charles pointedly recounted a dream in which he became an antibody which killed off all but one evil cell in an otherwise immortal woman, who went on to die in real life.

John Ward moved out to Scottsdale from London to join the group. 'What I need is to be with other people who have a commitment to me being alive,' he said. 'I need to be with people who are giving me the message I'm always going to be there. I feel young. I feel faster.'

Bible references: Genesis 3:19; 5:24; Psalm 49:7-14; 82:6-7; 89:48; 103:14-16; 146:3-4; Ecclesiastes 3:19-20; 9:2-6; John 8:51-3; Romans 5:12-14; 6:23; 1 Corinthians 15:22; Hebrews 9:27.

Source: Adapted from the *Sunday Telegraph*, 12 December 1993.

238. Cults – the Emin

(Commitment, Conditioning, Dancing, Human nature, Lifestyle, New Age, New Religious Movements)

In 1993, writer William Shaw joined the Emin, a home-grown British New Age cult, as part of an investigation of life inside the cults. He found it a strange and bizarre experience, as for example when the group went to Barbury Castle, a 2,000-year-old hill fort on the Marlborough Downs.

In the afternoon, we men are segregated from the women. It's the first hint of the range of sexual roles that we will gradually be allocated in coming weeks. The women are led away to learn Emin songs. 'Right,' says Matthew, 'we're going to do some exercises to reawaken the warrior in you.' I blink, horrified.

He lines us up in pairs and teaches us three marches, which he says come from ancient Iran. The first is called 'The March of the Friendly Negotiation', the second 'The March of the Alert Mind' and the third, 'The March of the Black Immortals'. Despite its name, the first turns out to involve stamping our feet hard on the soil in a most unfriendly fashion.... The idea of marching for an unseen world strikes me as absurd, even sinister. But as the strains of the girls' voices reach us we march, stumbling, out of step, while Lance bangs a drum to keep our raggedy steps in rhythm.... A pair of young punks gawp. I think I can hear them laughing. I wish they would go away and leave me alone with this humiliation.

As we copy Matthew, I catch Stone Bear's eye.... I can see he thinks this is as inane as I do. I strongly suspect we're not the only ones. But no one – out of all of us – dreams of protesting. I wonder what would happen if one of us stopped dead and said, 'I really don't like doing this?'

But no one does. As I parade up and down in the baking midsummer heat, I realise I am acting out a fundamental, depressing lesson about how cults operate. Once the collective has been formed, no one dares break ranks and say, 'Hold on. What we're doing is really stupid.' Once you've started tearing up reality, and rebuilding it in a different shape, you don't want to step out of line or the whole precarious structure will crumble.

Source: William Shaw, *Spying in Guru Land* (Fourth Estate, 1994), pp 37-8.

239. Cults – Hare Krishna

(Commitment, Dishonesty, Giving, Gullibility, Law, Lying, Money, New Religious Movements, Stealing)

Peter joined ISKCON (the International Society for Krishna Consciousness) when he was eighteen. For a couple of years he was involved in selling, mainly records. People were told that they could have the records free, but it would be appreciated if they would make a donation to help starving children or some other charity. Peter said, 'It worked a lot of the time – they gave generously. But sometimes there were punch-ups with born-again Christians and rednecks who knew that we were plain-clothes Krishnas. It wasn't really a scam, because the public got something for their money.'

He was arrested countless times, and sometimes held in cells overnight. The following morning his fine – for obstruction or selling without a permit – would be paid out of the takings, and he'd be out on the street again selling straightaway. 'There was a total disregard for the law. I did not mind – I thought every true believer was persecuted for their faith and tested by the "devil" in the shape of the police. I enjoyed life for a while and I was collecting £800 to £1000 a week.

'The Krishna women at this time were particularly successful at raising large sums of money. The main way was selling "smiley face" badges: they told a great variety of lies to persuade the public to part with money. What the public who bought the stickers were never told was that the face was modelled on that of Jagganatha, a Hindu god. One of their greatest successes was posing as Catholic aid workers when the Pope visited Ireland. Having sold out of all the plastic statuettes of the Pope that they had bought wholesale, one of them did a roaring trade selling leaves from a tree under which she claimed the Holy Father had stood. She made a fortune.'

Source: Adapted from Jean Ritchie, *The Secret World of Cults* (Angus and Robertson, 1991), pp 63-5.

240. Cults – Jehovah's Witnesses

(Bible study, Clergy, Commitment, Freedom, Guilt, Lifestyle, Love, New Religious Movements, Sects)

Eddie Cooney was in his twenties when two Jehovah's Witnesses knocked on his door. They seemed pleasant, and Eddie was interested by what they said and what they showed him in the Bible. He studied the literature they gave him, despite the warnings of his Irish Catholic parents, and in the end invited a Roman Catholic priest round to discuss the Bible with them. Eddie says, 'I'm afraid they just tore him to pieces, quoting the Scriptures at him. It was not a pleasant evening, and the priest ended up storming out.

'So after that I started going to Kingdom Hall. I was welcomed, and I felt then that Jehovah's Witnesses were living as Christians; they were zealous, sacrificial and they were not making money out of it. I got rid of my insurance policies – after all, I wasn't going to need them in paradise, was I? I gave up my full-time job and started window cleaning, so that I had time to go from door to door.... Whenever I did see any of the family I drove them crackers trying to convert them.

'But after a while, the initial sense of freedom and love vanished. That's typical of cults – but by then you are trapped. I had a tremendous sense of guilt; no Witness can ever work hard enough. I had meetings to attend, *Watchtower* material to read, door-to-door work to do. I gave up my freedom of choice, freedom of thought. I learned not to trust other people: we were constantly being told not to trust anyone "of the world", which was evil.... A great deal of time was spent at the Kingdom Hall discussing who was "weak". One lady had to leave early to get her bus home, but that was regarded as weakness.'

In the end it was Eddie's wife Anne who made the break. At first Eddie was shocked, but her stand made him ask the elders questions about the movement, questions which they seemed reluctant to answer. The final confrontation came when he and two other Witnesses who were having doubts met with two elders to discuss various Biblical interpretations. This time it was one of the elders who stormed out, as the Catholic priest had done ten years earlier. Eddie left the Jehovah's Witnesses, a decision he has never regretted.

Bible references: Galatians 1:6-9; Colossians 2:8; 1 Timothy 6:3-5, 20-1; 2 Peter 2:1-3; 1 John 4:1-3; 2 John 1:7-11.

Source: Adapted from Jean Ritchie, *The Secret World of Cults* (Angus and Robertson, 1991), pp 153-8.

241. Cults – the London Church of Christ

(Busyness, Church, Commitment, Conditioning, Discipleship, Dishonesty, Evangelism, Exclusiveness, Freedom, Lifestyle, Love, Preaching, Sects)

Karl Williams was a member of the London Church of Christ for a while in the late 1980s. Here he describes what drew him in, what he found once he was a member, and the struggles he had in getting out again.

> When that polite young man from the London Church of Christ stopped me in Acton High Street and simply asked if I was interested in some meetings they were having, I took the leaflet, a little suspicious but curious none the less.... The regular phone calls I received, the invitations to social events and the unbelievably pleasant nature of many of the individuals encountered, encouraged me to become a member. So too did the preaching, which was frank and forthright....
>
> However, not all was entirely as it seemed. The outward show of warmth and affection masked what was occurring behind the scenes. The church preferred to keep much of what it believed and practised hidden from outsiders. They didn't, for example, tell visitors that the London Church of Christ organisation considers itself to be the only truly Christian church, that all others are damned for eternity, and there is an unspoken agenda to convert everyone who attends. Neither were its leaders forthcoming with their

new recruits. They consistently failed to explain the full extent of the commitment – whether personal, practical or financial – that was required of them, or the level of control which leaders expected to exercise over their lives....

Each recruit is given a 'Discipler', a spiritual shepherd.... I was told that I should obey him in all things even when I strongly disagreed with his advice. To refuse was tantamount to disobeying Christ himself.

I was also told I was required to attend three meetings a week.... It soon became clear that what was actually expected was considerably more. On evenings when there were no official meetings, informal events were arranged. A quiet night in was not an option. Members were expected to use their time productively; at the very least they should spend an hour out on the street or on the London Underground evangelising....

Leaving the Church of Christ wasn't easy. It took me about a year to finally make up my mind to go. No one prevents you from walking out but members are constantly told about those who 'fall away', the miserable lives they are supposed to lead and the eventual damnation that they will face. I was telephoned regularly any time from eight in the morning to gone eleven at night. Members would turn up on my doorstep and other places, but they soon lost interest when it became clear I had no intention of returning.

Bible references: Matthew 11:28-30; 23:4; Galatians 5:1; Colossians 2:20-3.

Source: Quoted in the *Daily Telegraph*, 8 October 1994.

242. Cults – the Order of the Solar Temple

(Exclusiveness, New Age, New Religious Movements, Pride, Salvation, Suicide)

A Canadian insurance salesman who joined the Order of the Solar Temple, the secretive New Age group which apparently committed mass suicide in Switzerland in 1994, explained the cult's appeal:

> You become disengaged and disconnected from everything that surrounds you, and there's only one key to your life's purpose or your life's objective, and that's in the Solar Temple. That's where it's at, that's where it's going on, and nothing else really matters. It flatters your ego to be part of a group that designs itself as an élite, that are the chosen ones – how can you not feel good about it? I actually believed that I was superior to most other people on this planet, that I had been chosen, and I would start considering other people as being less than I was, not aware, not awake, having no idea of what life was really all about. So there was no other option for me than to stay within the group, because that's where my salvation was.

Source: Channel Four, *Witness*, September 1996.

243. Hypnosis

(Alternative Medicine, Health, Trance)

Two seventeen-year-old drama students at York College of Further and Higher Education thought it would be good fun to be hypnotised by a college friend of theirs. The problem was that once the hypnotist had put the two girls in a trance she found herself unable to rouse them again. The two were eventually taken to hospital, looking like 'zombies' according to other friends who tried unsuccessfully to wake them. Doctors summoned a hypnotherapist, who brought the girls out of their trance by rehypnotising them to cancel the effect of the first hypnosis.

The incident added to popular fears about the dangers involved in hypnosis. A helpline after a BBC programme about the dangers of stage hypnosis received 450 calls from viewers, many of whom claimed to have suffered unpleasant effects after they were hypnotised.

Source: Adapted from *The Times*, 6 October 1994.

244. New Age

(Angels, Books, Counterfeit religion, the Devil, Evil, Faith, Modern life, Religion, Sin, Spirituality)

The booksellers WH Smith have now introduced a 'Personal Development' section in most of their bookshops. The reason is purely commercial; as the executive buyer in charge of the area said, 'Anything in the spiritual or meditation line sells.' It's a trend that has crossed the Atlantic: spiritual books are regular features of the *New York Times* paperback bestseller list, and often sell well in hardback too. The American publishers Warner Books offer one explanation: 'It has a lot to do with a wealthy industrial society in which the one thing that seems to unify us these days is that there's a spiritual void in our lives.'

These are not books about Christianity or any other established religion, but works describing near death experiences and angelic encounters, or concerned with personal spiritual growth. As *Times* writer Kate Muir observed, 'The faith expected of readers is of an undemanding, semi-committed nature, without the effort required of mainstream church life. Nor do most of these books have a dark side: Satan and the wages of sin tend to go unmentioned. Welcome to the saccharine universe of New Age theology.'

Bible references: 2 Timothy 3:1-5; 4:3-4.

Source: Adapted from *The Times*, 16 August 1994.

245. Superstition

(Belief, Counterfeit religion, Despair, Faith, Hope, Luck, Modern life, Money, Neighbours, New Age, Prayer, Promises, Wealth, Wishes, Humour)

'A new Church report concluded that people are increasingly turning to superstition and a "pick-and-mix" attitude to religion. A browse through the advertisements in *Old Moore's Almanack* shows, in an often rather creepy way, quite how true this is. Rarely have I seen more queasily convincing evidence for the famous dictum that when a man stops believing in orthodox religion the danger is not that he will believe in nothing, but that he will believe in anything....

'At a time of increasing rootlessness, it is noticeable how many piskies and wishing stones and third eyes and mantras are advertised as coming from a definite locality. A pendulum is from Egypt, a Honey Charm from Tibet, a talisman from

Qabalah. A Miracle Cross of Fatima comes with real soil stuck to its back. Something billed as the Stonehenge Wishing Stone ("Many say the stone tingles in the palm of the hand as the wish is made") comes not, alas, from Stonehenge but from an unnamed "ancient stone circle"....

'A fair number of offers stem from the same source, a woman named Marie Simone from Totteridge. Not only does Marie Simone advertise a Lucky Golden Rabbit's Foot ("When you want to buy a new car, simply rub the GOLDEN RABBIT'S FOOT") and the Miracle Cross of Fatima ("the power of Fatima has taken America by storm") but also a bountiful statue of the Buddha ("How much money do you really want? £100, £1,000, even £100,000 or more? Don't be shy. Just name the amount.... Take the BUDDHA into your right hand and gently rub his magic belly") and an unspecified object called the Problem Solver. "The Mercedes I've always wanted was recently delivered right to my front door – paid in full," she reveals, and, even more mysteriously, "My mother is no longer a problem and to celebrate we went for the best second honeymoon ever!"

'Many advertisements appeal to those with irksome neighbours. "Heal a sick animal! Win a court action! Make a neighbour move away!" promises an ad for "Finger Magic", and a book called *100 Magic Prayers* includes prayer no. 68, "develop green fingers", prayer no. 23, "securing a bank loan", and – hey presto – prayer no. 5, "ridding oneself of a pestering neighbour".

'But beneath the absurdity, one catches glimpses of lives lived in a desperation so intense that even a lucky Golden Rabbit's Foot can be entertained as a possible cure.... Small wonder that the churches sense something is wrong.'

Bible references: 2 Timothy 3:1-5; 4:3-4.

Source: Craig Brown, in the *Daily Telegraph*, 16 November 1996.

246. Unlikely Messiahs – Hong Xiuquan

(Bible, Christ, Cults, False prophets, History, Kingdom of God, Lifestyle, Sects, Visions)

In the mid-nineteenth century, Hong Xiuquan declared himself to be the younger brother of Jesus Christ, raised an army of a million men, and established a vast kingdom in eastern China, stretching from Nanjing in the north to near Canton in the south. Hong was a failed Civil Service candidate who had been influenced by Christian missionaries from Canton in his youth. He claimed to have had a vision in which he was taken up to heaven and told by God that it was his task to create the kingdom of God on earth, following biblical principles.

The style of this kingdom was communal and puritan: property was held in common, alcohol and opium were banned, adultery was forbidden, and there was strict segregation between the sexes. Although his decrees were often issued in biblical language, Hong rewrote parts of the Bible he didn't agree with, such as the story of Noah's drunkenness and Jacob's cheating of Esau. He even named one of his generals 'the Holy Ghost'.

When a British gunboat was sent upriver from Shanghai to Hong's capital at Nanjing, Hong took advantage of the opportunity to ask the captain a series of questions about God which he was sure the British could answer, as they had been worshipping God for far longer than he. In particular, Hong wanted to know God's attributes – his height, his width, the size of his abdomen, etc – but Captain Mellersh, having held an emergency 'synod' of his crew members, replied that he was regrettably unable to oblige, as God did not have physical dimensions.

At the height of his popularity and power, Hong Xiuquan sent an army to capture the imperial capital at Peking, but the attempt failed. As the years passed, he become more interested in his role as son of God than in defending his earthly kingdom, the imperial forces rallied, internal dissent grew, and Hong found himself besieged in Nanjing. When food ran out and the people were starving, Hong assured them that God would send manna from heaven. To prove his faith, he ate some weeds from his courtyard, whereupon he died, and his bizarre vision with him.

Bible references: Genesis 9:20-7; 27; Matthew 7:15-20; 24:5, 23-4; Mark 13:21-2; Luke 6:26; 17:23; 21:8; John 6:30-1; 1 John 4:1.

Source: Adapted from review of Jonathan Spence, *God's Chinese Son* (HarperCollins, 1996) in the *Daily Telegraph*, 1996.

247. Unlikely Messiahs – Ron

(Christ, Disillusionment, End times, False prophets, New Age, Humour)

In 1976, a young bearded man named Ron kept turning up at the *Los Angeles Times* building asking for an interview with the religious news reporter, Russell Chandler. When Chandler sent a messenger down to send the man away yet again, Ron said, 'This may come as quite a surprise to you; I am the Messiah.' 'Well,' the messenger replied, 'this may come as quite a surprise to *you*, but you're the third Messiah we've had here today.'

Bible references: Matthew 24:5, 23-4; Mark 13:21-2; Luke

6:26; 17:23; 21:8; 1 John 4:1.

Source: Adapted from Russell Chandler, *Doomsday* (Word, 1993), pp 245-6.

INDEX OF STORIES

BIBLICAL INDEX

273

KI MPR